A Short Guide to Divorce Law in Ireland

A Short Guide to Divorce Law in Ireland

A Survival Handbook for the Family

HELEN M. COLLINS

First published in 2014 by Atrium
Atrium is an imprint of Cork University Press
Youngline Industrial Estate
Pouladuff Road
Togher
Cork
Ireland

Text © Helen Collins 2014
Graphics © Tom Halliday 2014

British Library Cataloguing in Publication Data
A CIP catalogue record for this book is available from the British Library.

ISBN: 978-1-909005-93-8

Printed in Malta by Gutenberg Press Ltd
Typeset by Cork University Press

For all Atrium books visit www.corkuniversitypress.com

Contents

Acknowledgements   vii
Preface   ix

1. Breakdown of a Relationship or Marriage:
   the bereavement process   1
2. Your Needs: Where to live? Your family home and the law   7
3. The Children: how do you tell the children
   about the separation?   15
4. Choosing your Lawyer: who do you want as your
   'family' lawyer?   19
5. Family-focused Options: do you want to go to court?   23
6. Urgent Court Applications   31
7. Court Applications if Agreement Cannot be Reached   35
8. A New Girlfriend/Boyfriend: where do I stand now?   39
9. My Child is in Trouble   43
10. Formalising Separation/Divorce: what do I need to do
    in terms of the law   48
11. Going Forwards: building a new life   59
12. Blended Families: here to stay   62

Top Ten Tips to Hang on the Fridge   67
Appendix A: Support Organisations and Registered Bodies   69
Appendix B: Costs Package for Collaborative Practice   73
Appendix C: Collaboratively Trained Lawyers   77
Glossary   85
References and Works Cited   89
Index   91

I dedicate this book to my mother,
Betty Collins, who personified love,
and to my children,
Kate, Eoghan and Jennie,
who carry that torch into the future

Acknowledgements

I am deeply grateful to my teachers, trainers and colleagues in the International Academy of Collaborative Practitioners: thanks to Dr Susan Gamache, psychologist; Jemima Brookman, psychotherapist; and Adele Plant, art therapist.

I have greatly benefited from the constructive feedback I received from Patricia Mallon, solicitor; Miriam O'Regan, barrister at law and family specialist; Nora Rice, solicitor; Colette McCarthy, solicitor; Susan Boland, social worker (retired); Kay Newman; Elizabeth O'Sullivan; Rachel O'Keeffe; and my sincere thanks to my editor, Gloria Greenwood.

The compelling graphics were created by Tom Halliday.

Preface

This is a short handbook on what to expect when your relationship with your partner or spouse breaks down irretrievably. I am writing this in the true hope that it will be of help and comfort to you, and will provide you with the information you need to empower you to make good decisions for you and your family. At a time when you may feel that your world is falling apart, I hope that it will guide you through this devastating chapter in your life and help you believe that you can come out the other end.

This handbook is not intended as a complete or comprehensive examination of the subject but as an immediate reference point in a fraught and difficult situation. There are already many wonderful books in existence on relationship breakdown. However, when someone is very distressed and in crisis it can be hard to concentrate or to read extensively and it is then that clear, accessible, concise and straightforward information can be invaluable.

I encourage you to read the book slowly and you may find it useful to read it a number of times. You may find it beneficial to discuss it with a close friend or family member.

In times of crisis it is important for people to develop awareness of the strong emotions driving their behaviour. This little book is intended to support you in understanding the powerful emotional forces at play in the family, and thereby supporting the family to make better and healthier decisions for themselves.

Also included here are an outline of the legal options and an overview of the relevant law and the general view of the courts. As this is an overview only, it is important to obtain detailed legal advice from your solicitor in relation to your own particular circumstances.

I encourage professionals who work with parents who are about to or who have recently separated to read this book as it is supportive of their work in respecting the family and holding it in the centre of matters.

It really is possible to have an amicable divorce. People have achieved this. With your determination, and the positive support of your lawyer, family and friends, this is achievable for you too. Yes, you can find an equitable and reasonable solution with your former partner. Yes, you can succeed. And, yes, you will be able to dance with your former partner at your daughter's wedding!

The book is largely based on my thirty-five years of experience as a family lawyer and my more recent experience as a collaborative practitioner and mediator. I have drawn extensively on the knowledge and skills I have gained from my teachers and trainers and the excellent training materials so generously made available by them and the International Academy of Collaborative Practitioners.

My personal experience as a separated and divorced spouse and mother has also informed my views. I sincerely hope that you will find the content of this little book useful.

HELEN M. COLLINS
February 2014

1. Breakdown of a Relationship or Marriage: the bereavement process

It is very likely that it feels as if your world is falling apart, the ground is gone from under your feet. One hour you may feel OK, the next you are in floods of tears; you get it together again for a couple of hours and then you fall into a total rage. You can't remember things; you can't seem to get your work done. For a while you believe you can survive and then you collapse into sadness.

This is 'bereavement' and you are on the bereavement curve, an emotional rollercoaster. These feelings are totally normal and happen to most people experiencing relationship breakdown.

In Ireland we are very good at dealing with 'death' – and we understand the process of coming to terms with it. We have all

heard the widow/widower being advised not to make any big decisions for a year or two when they are first bereaved. Scientifi-
cally, medically, psychologically and sociologically, it is recognised
that separation/divorce is a full-blown bereavement.

A person undergoing the bereavement process of breakdown
and separation is trying to survive, on both an emotional and
practical level. You will need to be able to support your children
emotionally and practically while at the same time making some
of the most important decisions of your life at a time when you
may feel least able to make those decisions.

It is important to recognise the strong emotions of bereavement, grief and loss and understand the effect they may be having on you. The five stages of grief and bereavement are:

1. *Denial.* We refuse to believe what has happened. We are
in shock.
2. *Anger and Fear.* We get angry. We may blame others for
our loss. We can have emotional outbursts. We may turn the
anger inwards on ourselves. It is important to release this
anger in a healthy way. Bad uncontrolled behaviour is often
caused by fear. Fear is common in grief. Violent and confus-
ing emotions, panic and nightmares, may make grief a fright-
ening experience. You may fear 'losing control' or 'breaking
down'.
3. *Bargaining and Guilt.* We may bargain with ourselves or,
if we are religious, with our God. We may try to make a deal
to have our loved one back. It is only human to want things
as they were before. Guilt or self blame is also common during grief. Regrets often take the form of 'if only's: 'if only I
had done this' or 'if only I hadn't said that'. It is common
also to feel a sense of relief or freedom, particularly if there
has been a lot of unhappiness and suffering in the relation-

ship, and this may also cause intense feelings of guilt.

4. *Grief and Depression.* We may experience feelings of list-lessness and tiredness – wandering around in a daze and feeling numb. Pleasure and joy can be difficult to achieve. There can be thoughts of suicide. If you have any thoughts of harming yourself, it is essential that you get immediate professional help. Self-preservation during this process is a must.

5. *Acceptance.* This is the final stage of grief. It is when we realise that life has to go on. This stage can take any amount of time to get to and varies with different people.

Write out the following list on a sheet of paper and hang it on your noticeboard or fridge to remind yourself that your feelings are totally normal and natural and that you will travel through these feelings.

FEELINGS OF GRIEF AND LOSS
Disbelief
Shock
Longing and searching
Anger
Guilt
Despair and hopelessness
Depression
Anxiety and fear
Loneliness and sadness
Relief
Physical reactions

It may be that the separation has come about due to one of you having an 'affair'. This is difficult to deal with. If you are the partner who had the affair, you may be experiencing deep feelings of guilt and shame. The affair may be a stark and public rejection of a marriage but for both of you it is important to understand that it is rarely the first sign of trouble in a marriage. Happily married couples generally don't engage in secret extramarital affairs.

If you are the partner learning of this affair, you may experience feelings of shock, humiliation and betrayal. The hurt of this betrayal may leave you struggling to let go of the desire for revenge. It may feel very difficult to work at co-parenting with your partner in these circumstances.

It is essential to focus strongly on your children's need for a healthy relationship with both parents. Your children did not hurt you – so do not hurt them by letting your own pain create obstacles to their relationship with your partner. Remember the saying: 'Holding on to anger and resentment is like drinking poison and expecting someone else to die!'

Obtaining the support and assistance of a professional counsellor is invaluable. Family and friends are great supporters but we all consciously and subconsciously censor what we say to our family and friends. We don't tell our mother a certain thing because we might cause her worry and she wouldn't sleep! We might not tell one friend 'X info' because he/she might disapprove and we don't tell another friend 'Y info' because he/she might be loose-tongued, and so on. One of the best services that you can ever do for yourself is to find a professional counsellor that you like.

You can speak to your counsellor without fear of judgement and with guaranteed confidentiality. Your counsellor will help you to deal with your strong feelings, assist you in being a positive support to your children and help you develop a means of constructive communication with your partner.

It is important to understand that very often families and friends are not good advisers – they have their own opinions, coloured by their own perceptions and biases, and may have difficulty in being objective. Their views can be driven by fear for what they perceive to be your well-being and this can be misguided. Do not let a family member dictate how you should behave towards your former partner – this can be very destructive for your children and your ongoing co-parenting relationship.

Get suitable legal assistance. (This is essential if you have real fears for your safety and your children's safety.) You can ask your family and friends for their love and support while also asking them to respect your need to obtain advice from an objective, reputable professional source.

It is very important to choose the professional assistance, particularly legal support, that best meets your needs and the needs of your family and your ongoing co-parenting relationship with your ex-partner. Difficult as it may feel at this time, it is vitally important to understand that your children need the love and attention of both parents. It is essential to try to maintain a working parental relationship with your former partner.

Try to do the following:
- Understand that your feelings are normal and that you are undergoing the strong emotions of bereavement.
- Get the assistance of a counsellor, who should be a registered accredited therapist (see Appendix A).
- Get suitable professional assistance.
- Make a conscious effort to take care of your mental, emotional and physical health.
- Support and actively encourage your children's love of the other parent and do everything in your power to facilitate regular access.

Try not to do the following:
• Hold up the world on your own (it will exhaust you).
• Talk to the children in a negative way about your former partner (see Chapter 3).
• Involve the children in any dispute (see Chapter 3).
• Be careless in the words used to explain to the children any departure or separation. Try to plan a joint and supportive approach for the children (see Chapter 3).
• Neglect yourself. If you don't put 'petrol' in your own tank, you can't drive anywhere! Furthermore, if you don't take care of your own physical, mental, emotional and spiritual welfare, you won't be able to healthily take care of your children's needs at this difficult time.
• Overdo your intake of alcohol. Alcohol can make strong feelings more difficult to handle. Consciously try to take daily exercise, good nutrition, fresh air, relaxation/massage, vitamins and minerals and generally support your nervous system through this very emotional time.

2. Your Needs: Where to live?
Your family home and the law

You may feel that you cannot stay together under the same roof any longer – it's all just too difficult and you want out. Or it may be that this talk of separation has come as a complete shock to you and you are devastated. It is important to realise that you and your partner are likely to be experiencing two different realities. One of you may have been thinking of separation for some time. The other of you may never have thought about it and may be shell-shocked when their partner announces that he/she is leaving. One person may be ready to go and the other person needs time to 'catch up'.

This emotional crisis will make it very difficult to make decisions. You may be the one who is ready to leave and you may be feeling frustrated with the slow pace of events. You may feel that your partner is dragging his/her heels or being obstinate and you may underestimate the effect of the separation on the children. Or you may be the person who feels that things are going too fast, who wants to talk more about the relationship and why the separation is happening, and may tend to overstate how angry or upset the children are with the person leaving.

It is very likely you are struggling to talk to your partner about your needs and that you are feeling that he/she is not hearing a word you are saying.

When we experience very strong emotion, we can get overwhelmed or 'flooded'. It is a scientific fact that when this happens our frontal lobe shuts down and we go into survival mode. We lose the ability to think rationally. Our heart rate increases and our body goes into red alert. We get flooded with adrenalin and we go into fight, flight or freeze mode. Most people feel intense fear or anxiety or anger. They experience a feeling of being swamped, a general sense of system overload. When flooded, we simply cannot think straight. It takes at least twenty minutes for any clarity to return to our thinking. If the stressful situation remains, our heart rate will remain elevated, our body will pump out adrenalin and our thinking will be clouded.

We talked about the emotional rollercoaster (the bereavement curve) in Chapter 1. Our human inability to function cognitively in a highly charged emotional situation, coupled with each partner's differing realities, makes for distressingly difficult circumstances in which to hear and respectfully respond (as opposed to 'react') to each other, and to endeavour to make important decisions. Some clients have described this to me as living in a parallel universe. The support of your counsellor is crucial and this is where a 'coach' and/or a 'mediator' can play a transformative role (see Chapter 5 for more details).

It is important to remember that you do not have to make lasting decisions in this highly charged situation. All your decisions can be made 'for the present moment' and can be agreed to be reviewed in a month or three months or six months' time. This is a new and very challenging situation for the family and it will take time and experience for both parents and the children to figure out what works best. Allow yourself this breathing space and try to keep an open mind.

Who is going to stay in the family home? Who is going to pay the mortgage? Where will the children live? When will they be with Mum? When will they be with Dad? All of these deeply emotional questions can be approached on a 'for the moment we can agree' basis, which gives you and the children time to acclimatise to your new situation.

A trained neutral financial specialist can be an invaluable support to a family in this traumatic transition stage and can help the family to prepare for the ongoing expense of two households (see Chapter 5 for more details).

BRAINSTORMING

Try using the technique of 'brainstorming'. This is a process used by successful organisations or businesses to develop a fertile environment for creative thinking and for developing options. You and your partner, supported by your lawyers and financial specialist, can use this process to open up all available options and solutions. It is important to remember that the first stage of brainstorming does not involve judgements or evaluations – all conceivable options and choices are laid out on the table. It is only in the later stages of brainstorming that the options most suitable to you and your partner, and most workable for your family, are identified. Brainstorming can produce creative and innovative solutions for you, even in a situation which might initially feel insoluble or hopeless (for instance, a house can be split in two, which can give a sense of safety and peace for the moment).

Historically and stereotypically, the financial 'power' (as the breadwinner) often rests in the man's hands. Conversely, the emotional 'power' (access to the children) often rests in the woman's hands. It is helpful to be aware of this. If you find yourself refusing to acknowledge your former partner's and your children's needs for access or their financial needs, the source of that refusal may be the need for power and control. The need for power and control is largely driven by fear.

When we feel stressed, frightened or threatened, we (if we are truly honest) are motivated by three desires:

1. The desire to be in control.
2. The desire to be right.
3. The desire to be the 'good' person.

Understanding what is driving us in any given situation will bring us more than halfway towards finding a workable solution.

Try to focus your thoughts on what you do want and not what you don't want; what you want for yourself and not what your partner wants or what you believe your partner will or will not agree to. In considering this, you will probably describe your 'position' – 'I'm the mother and I must have the family home'. However, you will need to look deeper and identify your 'interest'. Your interest is your underlying need: 'I need a safe and secure place in which to raise our children'.

'Interests' are creative and can be satisfied in lots of different ways. 'Positions' stifle creativity and can be satisfied in only one way. Your counsellor, coach or skilled family lawyer will be able to assist you in identifying your interests.

THE LAW AND YOUR FAMILY HOME

If you feel that conditions are such that it is impossible for you to remain in the family home (for instance, that it is unsafe), then the law will not penalise you for leaving. In law, this is called 'constructive desertion'. However, in practical terms it is important to note that if you leave the family home it may be difficult to physically get back into possession of the house. The courts tend to take the practical view that the longer you are out of the house, the harder it may be to get back in.

Your leaving the family home does not impinge on your right to claim a share in the ownership of the family home. If the family home is jointly owned, then you are entitled to a half-share in the property. If you are married and the home is in your sole name or in the sole name of your spouse, then the court will decide on the ownership share. The court has the discretion to make any property adjustment order and will take into consideration the length of your marriage, the health and needs of both of you, your finances and responsibilities, your earning capacity and if one of you is working in the home.

If the marriage has been a joint enterprise and of reasonably long length, then the court generally takes the view that each spouse has a half-share ownership in the family home. It is unusual for the court not to take this view (the marriage would need to be very short, have no children, and the non-owning spouse have independent means and not have contributed to the family home, etc.). Even then, the non-owning spouse may retain some percentage of the ownership of the family home. So, generally speaking, with some exceptions, it is reasonable to believe that the court will take the view that each spouse has a half-share interest in the family home, even if ownership is only in one spouse's name (see also Chapter 10, point 1).

If you are not married and the ownership of the home is in your sole name or the sole name of your partner, then the legal situation is determined by the Law of Equity or the Civil Partnership and Certain Rights and Obligations of Cohabitants Act 2010 ('the 2010 Act'), if this applies. The Law of Equity examines in detail the financial and other contributions made by you and your partner, and determines ownership based on this.

The Civil Partnership and Certain Rights and Obligations of Cohabitants Act has two parts. Part 1 covers the situation where a person has entered into a formal civil partnership, and part 2 relates to the situation where a person is not married, has not entered into a civil partnership and has been cohabiting for at least two years (if both are the parents of one or more children) or at least five years in any other case, provided that neither partner is married to anyone else or, if one is married, that that person has lived apart from his/her spouse for at least four years in the previous five.

If you are part of a registered civil partnership, then you have a number of legal protections under the 2010 Act. Instead of referring to a 'family home', the Act refers to a 'shared home'. The Act is very new and there are few court precedents available to date. However, I believe that it is most likely that the courts will respond in a very similar way to an application for dissolution of a registered civil partnership as they do to applications for separation/divorce. The court has the power to protect the 'shared home', to protect succession rights and pension rights, and to make property adjustment orders, maintenance orders, financial compensation orders, pension adjustment orders and other protections. Civil partners have similar capital acquisition tax protection to married couples.

If you are a co-habitant (not married and not a registered civil partner), then it is very important to establish if you are a 'qualified co-habitant'. If you are a qualified co-habitant, you have certain rights and protections under the 2010 Act. These rights are more limited in both nature and extent than those currently available to married couples and civil partners. The court can make certain property adjustment orders and, in so doing, could deal with the family home but must take a number of matters into consideration. These matters include both partners' financial circumstances, the rights and entitlements of any spouse or former spouse, the rights and entitlements of any civil partner or former civil partner, the rights and entitlements of any dependent child or of any child of a previous relationship, the length of the relationship, the degree of commitment to each other, the contributions made by both partners, the contribution made by either partner in looking after the home, each partner's earning capacity, any physical/mental disability and the conduct of each partner. Before the court makes a property adjustment order it must decide if it would be more practical to meet either partner's needs by way of a maintenance or pension adjustment order. The court may make redress orders if it is satisfied that you are financially dependent on your partner. Such financial dependence must arise as a result of either the relationship itself or the ending of the relationship.

Try to do the following:
• Be aware that you and your partner are experiencing two different realities and this is one of the reasons why communication is so difficult. It is most likely that you are not hearing each other. Do your best to really listen to what's being said.
• Be aware of the strong emotions (particularly fear) driving

your thoughts, words and actions.

• Make decisions for now – take baby steps! Big and permanent decisions do not need to be made immediately.

• Spend some time identifying your 'interests'.

• Get professional help and good legal advice (see Chapter 4).

Try not to do the following:

• To 'react'. Take things slowly and give yourself space to respond.

• To deliver ultimatums. This is driven by fear and is counterproductive.

• To take 'positions'.

• To be aggressive. All efforts made by you to listen and really communicate are hugely valuable for both you and your children.

3. The Children: how do you tell the children about the separation?

If at all possible, both you and your partner should tell the children together. Speak to them in a clear neutral tone. Try not to focus on your own feelings but instead focus on the children's feelings and needs. Do not turn the situation into something secret or hidden and make sure you allow the children to speak openly to both of you about their questions and concerns. Most importantly, try not to blame your partner.

Give sufficient information and answer your children's questions in as reassuring a way as you can. It is vital that the children are assured that Mum and Dad's love for them remains unchanged and that you both will always continue to be loving parents to them. Discuss practical information as to where they and each parent will be located, the availability of visits, etc. Children can sometimes blame themselves for a relationship breakdown, so be sure to reassure them that they are not at fault in any way. Depending on the ages of the children, discuss with them their needs with regard to informing their extended family, schools, teachers, etc.

Avoid talking to the children about the details of the relationship breakdown. They don't need to be dragged into the battle! What you are aiming to achieve is to be open, honest and reassuring with the children without straying into negative and destructive territory.

It is very important to acknowledge that, although your spousal relationship with your partner may be over, your co-parenting relationship is continuing on. Legally it continues until your youngest child reaches eighteen (or twenty-three if in full-time education; it will be lifelong in case of disability), but realistically it continues on for your lifetime. You should now be working at developing a new co-parenting relationship with your former partner.

It is fully established, and this is recognised and supported by the courts, that children need the love and attention of both parents. Children see themselves as half of one parent and half of the other parent. One of you may see yourself as the 'good and loving' parent and the other parent as deficient. You may believe that the children love you more. However, this is not generally the case, as children tend to love both parents equally regardless of bad behaviour on the part of one or both parents.

Research has established that, if one parent criticises, 'bad mouths' or attempts to downgrade the other parent, the children internalise this criticism as against themselves. Research has also established that the separation/divorce in itself does not necessarily cause harm to the children. The critical factor found in determining harm to the children is the behaviour of the parents.

A co-parenting relationship with a minimum level of conflict and a maximum level of cooperation between parents is what your child needs. No matter what age your children are, there will be ongoing everyday co-parenting needs. If you can achieve a practical co-parenting relationship with your former spouse and both of you can be parents together for your children through the separation/divorce process, through school, teenage problems, graduations, weddings, etc. – all the disappointments and the joys in your child's life – then there is no greater gift that you can give to your children.

Do your children one of the best services you can as a parent and:

- Love and support them unconditionally.
- Do not make them take sides. In this regard, beware of any subtle or understated behaviour on your part.
- No matter how upset you are and no matter how badly you view your former partner's behaviour towards you, do not criticise him/her to your children.
- Communicate directly with your former spouse on matters relating to the children.
- Fully and positively support your children's need to have full and free access to their other parent.
- Do not create obstacles to access (such as children's activities, homework, appointments, illness, etc.).

Please note that for the last two points above, of course, child protection and safety issues are excepted.

Try to do the following:
- Listen to your children
- Respect and support your children's need to have the love of both parents.
- As a minimum, speak in neutral tones in front of the children when referring to their other parent.
- Work at building a co-parenting relationship. Your children will really thank you for this.
- Be available for your children. Do not disappear!

Try not to do the following:
- Influence (subtly or otherwise) your children against your former partner and his/her family.
- Speak badly to your children about him/her and any member of his/her family.
- Sabotage in any way the relationship between your children and their Dad/Mum.
- Deny or obstruct an ongoing co-parenting relationship.
- Make your children carry messsages to your former spouse – communicate directly.

4. Choosing your Lawyer: who do you want as your 'family' lawyer?

Despite the fact that you and your partner are now separating or are already separated, you both remain the parents of your children and, as far as they are concerned, they and you – Mum and Dad – will always be a family. You may be losing your marriage but you are certainly keeping your family!

So, which kind of lawyer do you want to entrust your family to? In Ireland we have a Common Law adversarial legal system and this serves our democracy well in many important legal areas. However, the adversarial system means one person is in adversity against the other. When57
family relationships break down, it is a crisis for the fam-

19

ily. When this crisis situation is placed within the adversarial legal system, the process itself (despite the best efforts of the people involved) can be hugely damaging for the family. Our adversarial legal system is not a family-friendly system and should not be used to resolve family disputes unless there is absolutely no other option.

The problem is that we tend to be familiar with this legal system and, when we take up our 'positions' (rights and entitlements) and communication has broken down with our former partner, it can seem like the right course of action in order to force some form of resolution. We forget why communication has become so difficult, we forget to examine our 'interests' (our needs and the needs of our family – which includes our former partner) and we forget that fear and strong emotion are often driving our actions. If you feel the need to choose a 'Rottweiler' litigation solicitor to make sure you get your rights, it is very likely that you are experiencing deep fear. When your family urges you to engage such a solicitor, it is also very likely that their advice is coming from a very fearful place.

Of course, it is important that you choose a strong, skilled, experienced and supportive solicitor and it is essential that you secure a reasonable and proper outcome. Both our separation and divorce legislation require that 'proper provision' be made for each spouse, taking fully into consideration the needs of the children. Your solicitor has an obligation to ensure that you receive 'proper provision'. However, there are many ways to achieve that.

This 'proper provision' does not need to be obtained at the cost of the destruction of your ongoing co-parenting relationship. The legislature and the courts recognise this and the courts can now require mediation to take place. This situation will be strengthened by the Mediation Bill 2012 which is due to come before the Houses of the Oireachtas in 2014. Many highly experienced and skilled solicitors who recognise and support the need to safeguard the family and family relationships have now up-skilled to train as mediators and collaborative practitioners.

Court negotiation and court proceedings are not your only option. Collaborative practice and mediation are effective family-focused alternatives. You can very successfully engage in collaborative practice or mediation with the right kind of assistance and support.

CHOOSE YOUR LAWYER CAREFULLY

Check that your lawyer has trained in collaborative practice and is a trained mediator. These additional skills are hugely important to you, your family and your future. Don't sell yourself short (see Chapter 5 for further information on collaborative practice and mediation. See also Appendix C for the current list of CP-trained lawyers).

The Association of Collaborative Practitioners website address is www.acp.ie. On the website you will find an up-to-date list of practitioners in your area. Practitioners include family lawyers, coaches and neutral financial advisers. Initial contact can be made with any practitioner in your area.

The Irish Mediators Institute website address is www.themii.ie. They will supply you with a list of lawyers with mediation skills.

The Law Society of Ireland website address is www.lawsociety.ie. Contact them for:

- A list of lawyers with collaborative practice skills.
- A list of lawyers with mediation skills and specialising in family law.
- A list of lawyers with both the above skills.

Try to do the following:
• Consider options that are family focused.
• Engage a skilled and supportive lawyer who is family focused and has collaborative practice and mediation skills.

Try not to do the following:
• Seek retribution or one-upmanship through a 'Rottweiler' lawyer.
• Cut off your options.
• Forget that you are co-parenting for life.

The Legal Aid Board has trained a large number of their solicitors in collaborative practice.

5. Family-focused Options: do you want to go to court?

My experience is that almost everyone will say answer 'no' to the question 'Do you want to go to court?' Then why do so many end up in court despite this fact?

You may reply that you have no choice because your partner wouldn't cooperate. However, if both you and your partner (separately) were to be asked the question, both of you might give this answer. How can it be that each of you thinks the other is the reason for going to court? There are many layers to this, involving our personal experiences in life, our belief system, our awareness and much more.

Fear is often the driving force (remember the very strong bereavement emotions that we discussed in Chapter 1). Feelings of powerlessness, sadness and a fear that your partner will not respect your needs are often the catalyst for court proceedings. The legal management of the consequences of close relationship breakdown is called Family Law. If the truth be told, family breakdown is such a devastating experience that probably only 25 per cent or less has anything to do with law. When you realise this you can understand why the law and the courts cannot provide the level of resolution necessary for you and your family to find peace and move on in a healthy and positive way.

Nobody knows your family as well as you and your partner. Nobody is better placed to make decisions for your family. Why hand this power over to somebody else, such as a lawyer or a judge? A judge will tell you, faced with a long list of cases, that he or she will struggle to do their best to make huge decisions for your family, which he or she doesn't know, in the short time allotted for the case.

You do not have to go to court. The following are brief descriptions of other tried and tested options that are available to you.

1. *Collaborative practice*
This process recognises:
- That you and your former partner, with the right kind of support, are the people who can make the best decisions for your family.
- That you are feeling very strong emotions and you are struggling in your efforts to communicate; that you are sometimes feeling frightened, anxious and overwhelmed.
- That you want to ensure that the children's needs are fully met and you want to be the best parent you can be.

• That you want to ensure that the property and finances are fully disclosed and shared out in a reasonable way in the family.

This process can happen quickly and resolution can be achieved effectively without long delays in waiting to get to court. A set cost package is also available (see Appendix B).

In the collaborative process, you hire a trained collaborative lawyer and other collaborative professionals as needed to work together in an 'out of court', problem-solving, non-adversarial process. Instead of conducting negotiations between you and your partner by letter or telephone, you, your partner and your respective lawyers will meet together to work things out face to face. You will be assigned a 'coach' to assist you in this process. Your coach will have a therapeutic background and be a trained collaborative practitioner. Your coach, just like a sports coach, will help you, from the beginning of the process to the end of the process, to work constructively with your strong emotions, to build communication with your former partner and to work out arrangements that best meet your children's needs. When you meet with your former partner you will have your lawyer by your side throughout the process, so that you will have support and legal advice as you go. You will also have your coach by your side to help you to identify your needs and interests and to engage in productive and constructive negotiation.

A binding commitment is made by you, your partner and your respective lawyers to voluntarily disclose all relevant information and proceed respectfully and in good faith in settlement negotiations. Financial information must be fully exchanged and disclosed. The collaborative process offers innovative solutions and approaches to assist in reaching settlement. The collaborative lawyers will sign an agreement with you that disqualifies them from representing you in court if the collaborative process breaks down. This means they are absolutely committed to helping you find the best solutions through agreement rather than through conflict.

This is a reliable, open process which allows you and your lawyer to bring to the table whatever expertise is needed at that time. Usually, one neutral financial specialist is appointed to your case. This specialist collects all the financial information from both you and your former partner and assists both of you to examine this information carefully (so that you are both fully informed) and to work with this information in a constructive way towards a family-focused solution. If necessary, a neutral child specialist may be appointed to speak with the children so that their views and needs can be brought to the table.

This may sound like a lot of people, and accordingly may sound expensive, but this is not necessarily so. In fact this approach gives you exceptional value for money. The constructive and focused nature of the discussion soon highlights the problem areas. The right kind of expertise can be readily identified and applied, and that expertise is there only for as long or as short a time as is necessary. The emotional support of the coach can obviate the necessity of costly additional legal proceedings. A coach's fees are much less than legal fees and there is real value for you when you deal with the issues around your children with the coach.

There is a high level of client satisfaction with the collaborative practice process, as it supports a family-focused solution. It can be much quicker and less expensive than going to court, and a set cost package is available. This takes the worry of big court costs out of the equation.

2. *Mediation*

Mediators are especially trained to help people to resolve disputes. A mediator is neutral and will not take sides. Mediation is a voluntary process and can be an effective and immediate alternative to court proceedings. It is an entirely confidential service and provides a safe environment for people to air their issues. The mediator assists clients in finding a mutually acceptable solution to their difficulty. The format of the mediation process may vary, depending on the mediator and the type of dispute, but generally would involve both you and your former partner meeting together with one or two neutral mediators. It is not in itself a legal process and, generally speaking, a solicitor will not be present. However, there are variations available where solicitors may be present, by agreement with all parties.

The mediation process where a solicitor is present (particularly if the solicitor is trained to respect and engage constructively in this process) is, in my experience, a more all-round productive and effective process. Such 'lawyer-assisted' mediation has the potential to meet the family's needs, including legal resolution. Lawyer-assisted mediation is available through the following centres (see also Chapter 10 for more details):

- The West Cork Resolution Centre, Skibbereen (tel. 087 2137624; www.westcorkresolution)
- The Cork Resolution Centre, Sheares Street, Cork (tel. 021 4274018; www.corkresolutioncentre.ie)
- The Dublin Resolution Centre, 167 Lower Kimmage Road, Dublin 6W (tel. 087 185544; www.dublinresolutioncentre.ie)

There can be a long waiting list for the public mediation service. So far, the Cork Mediation Service (public) is not prepared to consent to having lawyer-assisted mediation. If you are pre-pared to engage in private lawyer-assisted mediation, then this can begin quickly, effectively avoiding long delays in waiting to get to court. A set cost 'package' is also available.

How will mediation benefit you?

- It is confidential.
- It is quick.
- It avoids the necessity of fighting in court and in this way protects 'relationships'.
- It is cost-effective.
- It gives greater scope for more creative and workable solutions.
- You and your former partner control the content and out-come, which supports the potential for longer-lasting solutions.
- Settlement potential is high.

3. COURT PROCEEDINGS

Court proceedings are based on an adversarial system, one side against the other. Separation/divorce proceedings must be heard in the Circuit Court or the High Court. You and your partner will engage separate solicitors and each of you will engage separate barristers. Each of you will also probably engage separate accountants and separate auctioneers (to value properties). A set collection of legal documents will be prepared by each side. You and your partner will not meet with each other to discuss matters. All discussions will be between the two solicitors and the two barristers, and you and your partner will not be present. You will probably wait in a separate room and your solicitor and barrister will report back to you.

When the case comes to trial, the judge will read the court

documents that each of you and your lawyers have prepared, will listen to short evidence from each of you (the judge will have at least six other similar cases on his/her list for hearing that day) and make as good a decision as he or she can in relation to your family.

The court procedure will be as follows:

• The court will make the decision (not you or your spouse).
• The court will not want to spend time on emotional issues.
• The court will work to ensure the children's well-being – the law requires this – and will generally try to ensure that the children have contact with both parents. The court will not support the exclusion of one parent unless there is a very compelling reason (e.g. murder). Even in established child abuse situations, strictly supervised access may be permitted.

The court will decide matters of access, maintenance, property division, pension division and other issues. From beginning to end, the process will take a minimum of nine to twelve months and often much longer. The costs will largely be decided by the level of conflict and the number of court appearances (i.e. the greater the level of conflict, the higher the legal costs).

4. LEGAL AID

In Ireland, legal aid is not available to engage private solicitors in the judicial separation/divorce Circuit Court proceedings. To obtain legal aid, you must be assessed by the Legal Aid Board and, if deemed suitable, you will then be appointed a solicitor from your nearest Legal Aid Board office. There are thirty-one Legal Aid Board offices in Ireland – eight in Dublin, two in Cork city, one each in Waterford, Westmeath, Limerick city, Tralee, Galway city, Wexford, Wicklow, Nenagh, Sligo, Tullamore, Monaghan,

Navan, Castlebar, Dundalk, Longford, Portlaoise, Kilkenny, Newbridge, Letterkenny, Cavan and Ennis – and four part-time centres, in Carlow, Bantry, Donegal town and Killarney.

If you qualify for legal aid, you cannot engage your own so-licitor; you must work with the legal aid solicitor appointed to you at your nearest Legal Aid Board office (although this may be as far away as sixty miles from you). It is important to note that, even though you have been awarded legal aid, your legal aid serv-ice will not necessarily be free. The only separation/divorce pro-ceedings that will be without cost to the applicant (i.e. free) is where there are no matrimonial assets at all. If you receive any set-tlement at all by agreement or order of the court, whether it is all or part of the family home or any other property or money, the Legal Aid Board will charge you legal fees (similar to a private solicitor) for the work they have done on your behalf. If you are applying for legal aid for separation/divorce proceedings, it is wise to check this out with the Legal Aid Board with regard to your own situation (see chapter 10 for more details on these options).

Try to do the following:
• Inform yourself of the options available.
• Engage constructively in the negotiation process in order to obtain the best result for you.

Try not to do the following:
• Enter into court proceedings without seriously studying other options. Your solicitor is required by law to inform you of these options and give you the necessary information.
• Dismiss other kinds of dispute resolution as not being suit-able. Keep an open mind. With the right kind of help, you both can do it.

6. Urgent Court Applications

You need urgent legal assistance if any of the following situations apply to you:

1. • If you are suffering from domestic violence.
   • If you and/or your children are in danger.
   • If your partner has threatened violence and you are in fear for your safety and/or the safety of your children.

2. If one parent has threatened or is threatening to take the child/children out of Ireland.

3. If your partner is attempting or is likely to sell property or raise money or place any loans on the property without your consent.

4. If it is likely that a judgement will be registered against your family home/property.

1. Please contact a Family Law solicitor immediately and he/she will apply to the District Court on your behalf for an immediate protection order and a date for a hearing for a barring/safety order.

If your former partner breaches the protection order (verbal threats are sufficient to constitute a breach), the Gardaí are obliged to act immediately and arrest him/her. You and your children do not have to suffer violence and threats, and it is essential to bring matters into the court and obtain the protection of the court and the Gardaí. Please see Appendix A for domestioc violence support organisations. Protective legislation is contained in the Domestic Violence Act 1996 as amended and cases are heard in the District Court.

If you are not able to pay a private solicitor, please seek urgent assistance from your nearest legal aid office (see Appendix A). There can be delays and waiting lists in obtaining legal aid assistance (the Legal Aid Board office will respond quickly to an urgent situation) and most private family law District Court practitioners will help you out on a Legal Aid Certificate or for a manageable fee, so it is well worth your while contacting your local family solicitor to enquire about urgent assistance.

A Legal Aid Certificate can be granted to a private solicitor in a District Court matter. This is different from the situation which pertains to Legal Aid in a Circuit Court separation or divorce situation, when legal aid cannot be granted to a private solicitor.

2. If one parent has removed a child from Ireland, it is essential to contact the Gardaí urgently and the Department of Justice (as the central authority under the Hague Convention).

If your former partner is threatening to take your child/children out of the country, it is essential to contact your solicitor immediately. If your child's habitual residence is in Ireland, then one parent cannot take the child out of Ireland without the other parent's consent or on an order of the court. If your former partner takes your child out of the country, it is known as a breach of the Hague Convention and the authorities here will contact the authorities in the state to which your child has been taken (provided that state is a signatory to the Hague Convention) and steps will be taken to bring your child home to Ireland.

If you are not married to your child's mother/father and you are not joint guardian of your child, then you will need to contact your solicitor urgently to seek immediate court protection. If any threat of leaving the country arises and the matter is before the court, the court will often retain custody of the child's passport. When things settle down and an agreement is reached, many parents are able to agree to specific holiday periods abroad, with the child/children being safely returned home after the holiday.

3. If your partner is likely to or attempts to remove money, sell property or raise loans/mortgages without your consent, contact your Family Law solicitor immediately. He/she will advise you on all the available steps necessary to protect you and your children. These remedies can include injunctions (in cases of emergency) and Land Registry protection.

4. If you and/or your partner owe debts to other parties and one or more of these parties is suing you/your partner for these debts,

a court judgement could be obtained against you and/or your partner and this could be registered as a judgement against your respective interests in the family home. In this kind of situation it is very important that you issue separation/divorce proceedings, as a matter of urgency, in order to protect your interest, as a spouse, ahead of the other judgements. Once the proceedings are safely issued and appropriate Land Registry protections are put in place, you can consider your other resolution options, such as mediation and collaborative practice.

Try to do the following:
• Get immediate professional assistance.
• Take the necessary steps to protect yourself and your children.

Try not to do the following:
• Be afraid to take appropriate action. There are a lot of very skilled and capable people available to assist you.

7. Court Applications if Agreement Cannot be Reached

IF YOU NEED FINANCIAL SUPPORT FOR THE CHILDREN

If you are seriously short of money to support your children, an immediate (time for service can be shortened if necessary) District Court application can be made by your solicitor seeking the payment of maintenance from your former partner to you. It will be necessary for you and your former partner to complete detailed affidavits of means (a sworn document) setting out what you own, your income from all sources, your debts and weekly/monthly outgoings. The judge will decide on a weekly/monthly figure of maintenance, taking all of the above into consideration.

Please note that it is essential that you contact your local Social Welfare Office and your Home Assistance Officer to make an early application for all applicable social welfare assistance. In certain circumstances the Department of Social Welfare will require you to seek a court order for maintenance from your former partner so that the department can recoup some of the payment that they are making to you.

IF YOU ARE NOT MARRIED TO THE MOTHER/FATHER OF YOUR CHILD

When a child is born to a married couple, both parents are automatically joint legal guardians of the child until that child reaches the age of eighteen. However, if you are unmarried, the situation is different.

Current Irish law still states that if a child is born to an unmarried mother, the mother is the sole legal guardian of that child. The father can become joint legal guardian if the mother agrees and a consent Statutory Declaration is signed by both of them.

If the mother does not consent, the father can apply to the District Court to be a joint legal guardian. Generally speaking, the court (all things being equal) is favourably disposed towards granting such an application. Even if you are not a joint legal guardian, you can still apply to the District Court for access to your child. The Minister for Justice has announced that he is preparing legislation to be called 'The Children and Family Relationship Bill' which will come before the Houses of the Oireachtas in 2014. The Bill will reflect the new Constitutional provision relating to children arising from the 2012 Children's Referendum. It proposes, among other matters, to give unmarried fathers automatic guardianship of their child if thay have lived with the child's mother for at least a year before the child's birth.

IF YOU ARE BEING REFUSED ACCESS TO YOUR CHILD/CHILDREN
Your solicitor can apply to the District Court on your behalf under the Guardianship of Infants Act to seek the assistance of the court on the matter of custody, access and the welfare of your child/children.

The primary consideration of the court is the welfare of the children: what is best for the children – not necessarily what is best for Mum or Dad. The court recognises and supports the child's need for a safe, stable, loving relationship with both parents and the court will require both parents to behave in a way that supports and encourages this. Remember – you chose your partner/spouse to be the mother/father of your child/children. He/she was good enough for you then and in the subsequent years of the child's/children's lives. The fact that you have now separated does not turn the other parent into a demon or less of a parent in the eyes of the court.

The court generally actively supports joint custody and joint parenting because in most cases it is established that this is best for the needs of the children. There would need to be serious problems with one parent for the court to reduce/restrict access. Even in the case of a violent/criminal parent, the court will consider access under supervision. The court will try to balance the need of the child to know and love a parent with the safety and protection of the court.

Try to do the following:
• Take an honest, balanced and moderate approach to your court proceedings.
• Prepare well with your solicitor and provide your solicitor with all requested information in good time.
• Engage constructively in negotiations and settlement talks.
• Recognise that court proceedings can be extremely stressful

and put good, constructive and healthy support systems in place for yourself.

Try not to do the following:
• Make the children pawns in the court proceedings.
• Seek revenge or punishment of the other parent.
• Be untruthful or exaggerate your evidence to obtain your desired result.
• Involve the children and do not discuss anything with the children unless the case involves a question of safety that requires to be communicated to the children.

8. A New Girlfriend/Boyfriend: where do I stand now?

You have been struggling hard to regain some balance and to adjust to being 'me' not 'we'. You have been doing your best to maintain a civil relationship with your former partner and work at co-parenting. Then you learn that your former partner has a girlfriend/boyfriend. This comes out of the blue and completely knocks the wind out of you. What is happening?

When a separation takes place and each partner is faced with the struggle to live a single life, this newfound freedom can sometimes lead to one partner going very quickly into a new relationship. This can happen for a number of reasons, not least that some people may find it very painful to be on their own and want to find love again.

This can impact hugely on the situation and can be very difficult for the children and the former partner. This should not be underestimated. It is very important to understand the impact this can have, as it is very likely to cause problems which will affect:

• The delicate balance of the fledgling cooperative arrangement with the former spouse.
• The children's confidence and sense of stability in their new situation.
• The partner in the new relationship's ability to be available for the children.
• Any legal negotiations taking place.

In a court context, a judge will often not allow contact between the new girlfriend/boyfriend and the children for a defined period of time until it can be shown that the relationship is actually serious and long-term. The court takes the view that new partners need to be introduced gradually and with great sensitivity.

Statistically, the odds are against the new relationship being successful if sufficient time and work has not been done by that partner to resolve the broken former relationship and develop awareness around any changes needed to build a successful new relationship.

It is important to understand the probable impact of a new relationship on the former partner. The separation itself may already have caused a great deal of shock. He/she may have been hoping for reconciliation. He/she may be finding it very difficult to adjust to the changed situation.

The arrival of a new girlfriend/boyfriend can be a shocking blow to the former partner. It can be the blow that brings home the reality of the separation to him/her. There will be strong feelings of being 'rejected'; of being 'replaced', not being 'good enough'. The question 'What has he/she got that I haven't got?' is often uppermost. There can be strong toxic feelings of failure and despair and a deep and horrible fear that they will lose their place in the family and that the children may like the new partner better than them.

These strong and destructive feelings, the effect of which cannot be underestimated, have the potential to derail all the good work done by you and your former partner to date. For the partner feeling they have been 'replaced', it is very important to know that this is not so. You will always be Mum or Dad to your children.

In Ireland we are good at appreciating the benefits of the extended family – grandparents, aunts, uncles and cousins. These are all connected to our children and, generally, we don't feel threatened by this and it does not make us feel less of a mother or father. We understand the saying that 'it takes a village to raise a child'. It is helpful (and far less stressful) to think of the new partner as part of this 'village'. It will grow easier if, in time, the former partner can meet the new partner and have a respectful interaction. This could be of valuable relief to everyone.

Please do not question the children about the new partner – they are doing the best they can to manage their own situation. The children will take their lead from you. If you can manage to behave respectfully, then this will free them from huge stress and worry and allow them to acclimatise to the new situation. The introduction of a new girlfriend/boyfriend always needs to be handled with great care and sensitivity.

To the new girlfriend/boyfriend I extend the strongest plea not to add to the conflict in the family. It is imperative not to interfere. Offering loving support to your new boyfriend/girlfriend does not extend to you laying your opinions, your advice, your strategies on the other partner and/or the children. Your intentions may be admirable but in doing this you are interfering where you should not. You are a newcomer to this family and a much longer and more committed relationship with the family is needed first. Be sure that anything you say is very constructive. This is a delicate and difficult situation, so please handle it diplomatically, generously and with great consideration. It is not unreasonable for the other parent to have concerns about your contact with his/her children. She/he does not know you. If your relationship is serious, it is really useful to have a meeting (supported by a mediator if necessary) with both parents to answer any concerns and develop a working relationship (see Chapter 12).

Try to do the following:
• Be conscious of the impact on the family.
• Work towards a measured and considered introduction to the family of any new partners.
• Help the children to acclimatise in a positive and supportive manner.

Try not to do the following:
• Rush blindly into a situation that will have major consequences.
• Force your children to 'be happy for you'. That's not their job. You are the parent and they are the children. Your focus and consideration must be on helping and supporting your children. It is not their job to help and support you.

9. My Child is in Trouble

Despite your best efforts, your child/children will suffer some anxiety and sadness in your separation. Children may display a wide range of emotions and express their pain and anger differently at different ages. They may turn anger and pain inwards and withdraw or turn anger and pain outwards and misbehave. Children can feel responsible for the break-up and they can have deep fears of being abandoned. A child may exhibit symptoms of physical illness or may actually try to behave perfectly, believing that their improved behaviour could save the marriage.

The separation can be very stressful and harmful to the children, particularly if it is a high-conflict separation, and may result in a child getting into trouble. The 'trouble' can take many different forms. Is your child misbehaving in school? Doing badly in school? Missing school? Being sick a lot? Not eating? Not sleeping? Bed-wetting? Not responding to your reasonable requirements? Not coming home at agreed times? Behaving too perfectly? Constantly sitting in front of the TV/computer? Drinking alcohol? Taking drugs? In trouble with the law? Suspended from school? Speaking abusively to you, or to his/her siblings? Speaking abusively to his/her teachers? Hurting himself/herself? Hurting his/her siblings? Getting into fights? Hurting animals? Behaving violently? Disinterested in life? The list is endless!

Please listen, listen, listen. Understand and have compassion. No matter how bad the trouble is, this is your child and this behaviour is a cry for help. Keep loving your child. Be available and stand up for your child. Try to put any personal upset or shame to one side for the moment and focus on the help your child needs. Provide trusted friends, support and counselling for your child. Keep to routines as much as possible. Actively support, love and communicate with your child. It is important to recognise that your disapproval is of the behaviour, not the child.

Children should not be turned into a parent's minder. They should not have to listen to the parent's problems or worry about them. Each parent should resist the urge to use the children as a replacement for the absent spouse. Parents need to develop their own adult sources of support. We should not be dependent on our children.

Try to work constructively with your partner to co-parent your child with love, support and understanding. Join forces to be the parents your child needs. Leave your personal difficulties aside for the moment. Your child will really benefit from your efforts to co-parent and support him/her together. Not only will your child appreciate it; the school, the Gardaí, the health services, the court, your entire community will also appreciate it!

You may just about be surviving yourself and you may be

struggling to keep going emotionally and financially. It may feel nearly impossible to face these difficulties. Don't despair. There is help available. Get good professional care for your child.

• The Health Service Executive must provide you with support and assistance if your child is under eighteen.
• A lot of schools have a counselling service. The head of your child's school will put you in touch with this.
• Contact your GP for assistance and referrals from him or her.
• There are a number of excellent psychotherapists available for teenagers. Please see Appendix A and check on the website www.counsellingdirectory.ie for information and referrals.

A counsellor/psychotherapist can be of great assistance to your child. Talk to the therapist about your child's safety but try not to intrude into any professional relationship between your child and his/her therapist, particularly if your child is a teenager. Respect your teenage child's boundaries. The therapist will help with advice in this regard.

Younger children struggling to deal with emotional and behavioural issues can be greatly assisted through recognised therapies such as play and art therapies. Art is a natural development activity for children and something they engage with in their day-to-day lives. Art is a way for children to communicate non-verbally and symbolically. As a therapeutic intervention, it can be especially useful for children who find it hard to express or show their feelings or discuss issues. Through art they can get a chance to express themselves without the use of words. Art and play therapy can encourage development, help young children process stressful experiences and give a child a sense of power, control and confidence.

Ensure that the therapist is registered with a fully accredited supervisory professional body. The following contacts may be useful:

- The Irish Association of Creative Arts Therapies (087 9921746)
- PT Ireland (Play Therapy Ireland) (01 8423006)
- The Irish Association for Play Therapy and Psychotherapy (IAPTP) (www.iapt.net)
- The Irish Association for Psychotherapy in Primary Care (www.iappcare.com)

It can be very stressful for a child to be trying hard to please both parents. It can be a wonderful relief for the child to be able to speak to a 'safe', neutral therapist without fear of judgement.

If your child is under eighteen and in trouble with the law, the Gardaí will usually deal with any offences under the Juvenile Liaison scheme. As well as being a Garda, a Juvenile Liaison Officer (JLO) can be a highly trained mediator and restorative justice practitioner. Talk to the JLO and ask for assistance. If your child is prosecuted in court, get a good solicitor to represent him/her. It is very important that the court is made aware of the pressures and difficulties your child is experiencing. If needs be, the court will request a probation report. Most probation officers are skilled, constructive and very supportive. Be sure to work with the probation officer and get all the help available. Make the call and get the support you need for your child.

Alcohol and drug addiction assistance is available through the HSE, through your local health offices (go to www.hse.ie and click on 'addiction services', which will access the local health offices and furnish you with a list for your particular area). Further information is available through www.alcoholireland.ie, which also gives a list of services available in your area.

Get good professional advice and support for yourself. Try and inform yourself fully. Proper information is vital for your support and survival, and for your child. Remember to keep yourself well and healthy. There are a number of courses available which can help parents to develop new skills, particularly in times of family crisis. The HSE offers a number of courses, and information about these can be obtained from your nearest HSE Family Services office. Check too with your local Family Resource Centre about its parenting support courses (see Appendix A for further details).

There are also a number of private parenting courses available. Your doctor, solicitor or your counsellor can give you information about these. There are tried and tested techniques available for us as parents to assist us in the parenting of our children. It is really worthwhile to learn these techniques. Continuing education and learning new skills is something many of us have to do in our work. It is equally important for us to do this in our parenting, particularly as our children grow into adolescence and take on the pressures of a changing world.

Try to do the following:
• Believe in the goodness of your child and stand by him/her.
• Actively support, love and communicate with your child, recognising that you disapprove of the behaviour, not the child.
• Work with your partner, if at all possible, to co-parent, support, love and guide your child through this difficulty and onwards.
• Get professional assistance both for you and your child.
• Inform yourself fully, develop your parenting skills and get good advice and guidance.

Try not to do the following:
• Condemn your child and let shame and anger stand in the way of your love and support of him/her.
• Blame the other parent; remember that it was you who chose him/her to be the mother/father of your child.
• Try not to lose heart; healthy love and support and the right kind of help is transformative!

10. Formalising Separation/Divorce: what do I need to do in terms of the law?

1. THE COURT

The law in relation to separation and divorce for married couples is contained in the Judicial Separation and Family Law Reform Act 1989, the Family Law Act 1995 and the Family Law (Divorce) Act 1996.

The Judicial Separation and Family Law Reform Act 1989 introduced the concept of 'no fault' in separation. If 'no normal marital relationship' has existed between you and your spouse for twelve months, then it is open to you to issue a Judicial Separation Civil Bill. The Supreme Court, in T.F. v Ireland (1995), took the view that it is not necessary to prove who is at fault for the break-up of a marriage nor is it necessary for the court to find either party at fault. You do not necessarily need to be living in separate residences. As this can be a complex issue, it is important that you discuss it in detail with your solicitor.

If you have lived apart from your spouse for at least four years in the preceding five years, then it is open to you to seek a divorce. You may, in fact, be living apart even if you both live in the same house. Again, you should discuss this in detail with your solicitor.

Court proceedings start with a Judicial Separation or Divorce Civil Bill. One of you is named as the Applicant (the one who is starting the legal proceedings) and the other is the Respondent. This legal document sets out all the reasons why the Applicant says that he/she can no longer live with the Respondent. It is a difficult document to give and to receive. The Applicant lists all the things he/she wants and generally this is an all-inclusive list.

Attached to this Civil Bill is the Applicant's affidavit of means (this is a sworn document, which is also required in the collaborative process and in lawyer-assisted mediation, but is not a sworn document in ordinary mediation) and a document called an 'affidavit of welfare', setting out all the particulars about the children. These documents are served on the Respondent by registered post.

If the Respondent refuses service (refuses to accept the registered package containing the documents), an application must be made to the court for substituted service (court leave to serve by ordinary post or perhaps personally). On receipt of service, the Respondent has ten days to file what is called an 'appearance' and a further ten days to file a 'defence'. If the Respondent does not do this, the Applicant can submit a motion to the court for judgement in default of appearance/defence. Usually the Respondent is given six weeks to comply. If nothing happens in the six weeks, the Applicant can file another motion and often the court will then give the Respondent a further six weeks. Should the Respondent not reply, the court case will proceed in his/her absence and judgement will be given to the Applicant.

However, this is not the usual situation. In most cases the Respondent does comply and he/she will then file his/her defence, affidavit of means and affidavit of welfare. Both affidavits of means will be closely examined and a number of questions may be raised on financial matters. If the necessary information is not forthcoming, or if there is a concern that assets are missing, an application called 'discovery' will be made to the court. This may or may not produce results. Valuations will be prepared by auctioneers for each side and accountants for each side will prepare reports. If there is a dispute about custody and access, assessments and reports may be produced by a child psychologist for each side.

Eventually, when everything is in place, a 'case progression' examination will take place and the case will be added to the list for fixing a date for trial. A number of contested cases will be fixed for the same trial date and your case will take its place on the list. You, your spouse, your solicitor and barrister and all your witnesses will be present at the trial date and you will take your chances that your case will be reached on the list on that day. If it is not reached (or is not settled), it will be adjourned to another date and you will all return on that date. From beginning to end, the entire process will take at least nine to twelve months at its speediest.

Each case has its own special ingredients. The judge has a great deal of discretion and it can be difficult, at times, for lawyers to advise their clients with any degree of certainty as to the likely outcome of their case. In general, if it has been a long marriage, a joint enterprise and contributions have been jointly made, the court will take the view that the assets should be divided reasonably equally between you both. The court will consider all the circumstances of your particular case, each of your incomes, your finances and your financial contributions and, in the case of non-adult children, the court will do its best to keep the children in the family home.

Your solicitor and barrister will do their best to negotiate a settlement and, if agreement is not reached, the court will hear arguments from both your barristers and possibly evidence from you and your spouse, and will decide accordingly. (See Chapter 2 in relation to the possible views of the court on the family home.) However, it is important to note that Irish Family Law is based on the principle of 'proper provision' and not on 'a yardstick of equality' (Supreme Court T. v T. [2002] and G. v G. [2011]).

In deciding what is 'proper provision', the court must have regard to the following:

- each spouse's income and earning capacity;
- their financial needs and responsibilities;
- their standard of living;
- both their ages;
- the length of their relationship;
- any physical or mental disabilities;
- contributions made by each to the marriage and, in particular, the degree to which the future earning capacity of one has been affected by working in the home;
- the accommodation needs of each;
- the conduct of each; and
- the rights of any other person affected, including a person whom either has remarried.

In deciding what constitutes 'proper provision', the Irish courts have stepped away from the 'yardstick of equality' used by the English courts, especially in 'big money' cases (for instance the case of T. v T. (2002), where a figure of one-third was used by Mrs Justice Susan Denham for the non-high-earning wife).

It is important to know that, even though you may have agreed all the terms of your separation or gone through a difficult court case to obtain your Order of Separation, when it comes to the time to apply for your divorce (after four years of living apart), the case can be reopened if your spouse is not prepared to consent. In the Divorce Referendum of 1995, this was the proposal compiled by our politicians and put before and endorsed by the nation.

The courts try to take a practical approach to this and, in an effort to achieve 'certainty and finality', take the view that, unless there is some very significant change in your circumstances (e.g. one of you is seriously ill or one of you has won the Euro millions!), the court will not reverse its earlier decision. This was confirmed in the case of G. v G. (2011) in the Supreme Court, in which the court referred to the question of inheritance. The court decided that 'assets which are inherited will not be treated as assets obtained by both parties in a marriage. The distinction in the event of separation or divorce will depend on the circumstances . . . the circumstances of each case should be considered specifically'. These are all complex issues that you need to discuss in detail with your solicitor and barrister. Each individual case is decided by the court on its own particulars and merits.

If you meet the separation requirement and if you and your spouse have agreed terms providing each of you with proper provision, and particularly once the court is satisfied that your under-age children are secure, then you can obtain a Divorce Order 'on consent' quite quickly. A Divorce Civil Bill setting out the 'consent' must be filed with the court. The matter will come before the County Registrar and will be put into the judge's next consent list. One of you must attend the court with your solicitor/barrister to give a very short sworn evidence of separation and confirming the agreement with your spouse. Your spouse's solicitor/barrister will consent and, once the court is satisfied that all legal requirements have been met (including any pension adjustment orders), your divorce will be granted. You are then free to remarry.

2. COLLABORATIVE PRACTICE

Part 1 of Chapter 5 deals with this subject in some detail. Collaborative practice involves a structured and supported series of meetings, involving you, your collaborative lawyer, your coach, your partner, his/her collaborative lawyer and coach and a neutral financial specialist (if needed), in which negotiations take place on all matters of importance to you and your partner, to include children, living arrangements, maintenance, bills, mortgages, property, inheritance, pensions, etc. Each of you completes a sworn affidavit of means setting out all your income, assets and liabilities. Support will be given to each of you to secure full knowledge and understanding of the overall financial picture. If the collaborative process ever breaks down for any reason, it is important to know that these affidavits of means will survive the process and will be produced in any subsequent court proceedings. If any income/asset is not disclosed, the court will take an extremely serious view of this.

Everybody will work together to support you and your partner through these negotiations in order to reach a workable agreement and a successful conclusion. Please see Appendix B for the set costs package available from the Association of Collaborative Practitioners Practice Groups, 'Resolution' and 'Pathways'. Check with your local collaborative practitioner for this set costs package. On reaching agreement, you and your partner's collaborative lawyers will write up a legal agreement for signature by both of you. Both lawyers will apply on your behalf to the court for your Judicial Separation Order/Divorce Order based on agreement through the collaborative process. This is the only exemption for the lawyers from their court disqualification. Should any matter of difficulty arise between you and your former partner in the future, you both know that you can return to 'the table' and the collaborative process to find resolution. It is a powerful process designed to meet all the needs of the family.

3. MEDIATION

Part 2 of Chapter 5 deals with this subject in some detail. The mediation process, in its traditional form, involves a series of meetings between you, your partner and a neutral mediator. Generally the mediator is not a solicitor or barrister and mediation is not a legal process. Legal advice is provided to you separately and outside the process by your solicitor and likewise to your partner. There is generally no communication between your solicitor and your partner's solicitor, and between solicitors and the mediator. This can give rise to its own problems, not least a lack of practical legal advice and a lack of common purpose. Some participants in this traditional format have expressed concerns of feeling unsupported or that they are participating in an 'uneven playing field'. Even for a very skilled mediator it can sometimes be difficult to support both participants in a situation where there is a bullying/threatening dynamic in the relationship.

When an agreement is reached, it is written down by the mediator and signed by you and your partner. This is not a legal agreement. You must bring this document to your solicitor who will go over it in detail with you. Sometimes there are legal questions and problems to be gone through. It is desirable that each participant receives legal advice throughout the mediation process. Sometimes this does not happen and you may discover that you have agreed to a matter without understanding the full legal consequences. This can mean that adjustments may be necessary. Communication/negotiations will need to take place between both your solicitors and, if these adjustments can be agreed, one solicitor will write up a legal agreement for the approval of the other solicitor and, on approval, it will be signed by both of you. Other legal documents, such as 'pension adjustment orders', 'deeds of transfer' and 'deeds of waiver', will also be prepared and signed. An application will then be made to the court for an Order of Judicial Separation or Divorce, whichever is applicable.

I have experienced a reluctance on the part of some mediators to participate in lawyer-assisted mediation. Lawyers, traditionally, have been seen as aggressive and high conflict and I can appreciate that this view gives rise to concern for mediators who are working hard to reduce conflict and achieve consensus. Large numbers of experienced family lawyers, recognising the essential need to support the family through the process, have trained in collaborative practice and mediation and have, and are developing, the skills to constructively and productively support their clients in and through the mediation process. In the same way that it could be argued that the law cannot resolve family disputes without full recognition of the family's emotional needs, it can equally be argued that the family mediation process cannot resolve family disputes without full recognition of the family's legal needs.

The involvement and participation of an appropriately trained family lawyer can only benefit the mediation process in, contemporaneously, providing essential legal advice, reassurance and support. The agreement reached will encompass all legal requirements, together with supporting documentation, thus protecting it from subsequent legal challenge or from foundering because of legal requirements.

SYNOPSIS OF THE DIFFERENT OPTIONS:

Court:

• The service of Court documents starts the formal separation process.

• A sworn Affidavit of Means is prepared and signed.

• Each person has their own accountant (if necessary).

• Close to or on the Court date, the lawyers try to negotiate an agreement.

• The couple do not meet to discuss matters – the lawyers do the talking.

• If no agreement is reached each party gives sworn evidence, both are cross-examined and a Circuit Court Judge decides on what will happen to the children, and family property and money.

• Judicial Separation/Divorce Order is made by the Court.

Collaborative Practice

• The couple, through their collaborative lawyers and coaches, start the formal process

• The couple, supported by their coaches and lawyers, meet to discuss and decide upon the family issues including the children, money and property.

• A sworn Affidavit of Means is prepared and signed.

• A neutral financial adviser will examine all finances (if necessary).

• When all information is gathered the couple make their own decisions about the family issues at the meetings.

• A legal Agreement is drawn up in the course of the meetings and signed by the couple.

• The legal Agreement is brought to Court and a Judicial Separation/Divorce Order is made, on the consent of the couple, by the Court.

Mediation in the Family Mediation Service:

• The couple separately contact the Mediation Service and start the formal separation process.

• The couple receive a date for commencement and both meet with the Mediator.

• A series of meetings takes place with the Mediator.

• A Statement of Means (not sworn) is prepared by each person.

• Each person gets separate legal advice from their own lawyer.

• Each person has their own accountant (if necessary).

• Generally speaking: the lawyers do not meet; the accountants do not meet; the views of the children are not obtained.

• When an agreement is reached the Mediator sends the agreement to each person's lawyer.

• One lawyer draws up a legal agreement and sends it to the other lawyer for approval.

• If approved the agreement is signed by each of the couple.

• The legal Agreement is brought to Court and a Judicial Separation/Divorce Order is made, on the consent of the couple, by the Court.

Try to do the following:

• Fully inform yourself of the various processes available to you.

• Choose and engage in a process which works best for you and your family.
• Engage fully and constructively in your chosen process.
• Get all the help and support that you need.
• Take care of your own physical, mental, emotional and spiritual welfare, as this is a very stressful time.

Try not to do the following:
• Involve your children. They do not need to know what is happening between you and your partner. If a child's view is needed, there is a safe process through the child specialist for obtaining this.
• Make your children take sides. Your children need both their parents and want resolution for both parents.
• Ignore any court documents. Denying/ignoring the matter has the potential to raise the level of conflict and could ultimately damage your case or you could find yourself not having a say in the decisions made by the court.

11. Going Forwards: building a new life

You have survived! There were many times when you didn't think you would and you have. It is important to allow yourself to feel and believe this. Much pain has been suffered, many difficulties have weighed heavily on you, many painful lessons have been learned and are still being learned and you have done your very best.

The work of healing your wounds needs to continue so that you can become an effective parent in your co-parenting role and so that any new relationship you may embark on is a healthy one. Bringing raw wounds to a new relationship will not bode well for the success of that relationship. The work you do in healing yourself is not only of huge benefit to your children; it is of crucial importance to you in developing peace and happiness in your own life, whether as a single person or in a new relationship.

This is an opportunity to have a fresh start, to write on a clean new page. It is time to dust off all those dreams you had that may have been 'mislaid' over the busy years. It is possible to turn the pain and trauma of divorce into an opportunity for personal development. In order to make a clean start we need to work at getting rid of those old wounds and all the baggage that we have been dragging around with us. Once again, get help, support and good advice for yourself.

We are very familiar with the word 'therapy' when it is used for services such as speech therapy, physiotherapy, etc. Psychotherapy is just another therapy. In the same way that we may need physiotherapy if we hurt a muscle or injure a limb, we can benefit from psychotherapy when we have suffered stress, strain and trauma. Psychotherapy aims to increase our own sense of well-being. In facing our fears and rebuilding our self-esteem, we blossom and grow, and then all things can become possible, limitations and restrictions can be overcome and a fresh commitment – to work, education, job opportunities and so much more – can become possible. A return to education can be daunting but tremendously exciting and productive. Look into all your options. It's a time of change and development and you can, with support, confidence and information, make it work for you.

There are many different kinds of support therapy. Be sure to seek out information on each form of therapy and decide which might suit you the best. Each registered body will be able to provide you with a list of practitioners in your area. Ensure that your counsellor is a registered accredited therapist with a recognised professional supervisory body.

Cognitive behavioural therapy (CBT) is a highly focused,

practical and short-term therapy. It can be a very effective support for helping us to break old habits of thinking and behaviour that may no longer serve us well. This kind of therapy can be very useful when making a fresh start. Family systems therapy emphasises family relationships as an important factor in psychological health (see Appendix A for a list of registered bodies).

Try to do the following:
• Believe in yourself and know that you are a good person doing the best you can.
• Continue your good work in healing yourself.
• Help yourself to blossom and avail of all the help you can get.

Try not to do the following:
• Believe you are a failure. There is no such thing as 'failure', only an experience waiting to teach us something we need to learn. Life does not give us a pass or fail; life continuously presents us with experiences from which we learn. This is the story of life and part of the purpose of our existence.
• Be hard or judgemental on yourself. We are human, with all the usual human strengths and weaknesses. None of us is perfect. You are human too.

12. Blended Families: here to stay

Back in the 1850s, the average length of a marriage was less than ten years. This was because people died in childbirth, wars, from disease, etc. Remarriage rates were very similar to those of today.

In 2014 the length of a marriage can be fifty years. Scientists suggest that the first person to live to 200 has now been born. What will this mean for marriage? The reality is that our life expectancy has changed dramatically in the last 150 years and will change even more dramatically in the next fifty years. Remaining married to the same person for fifty to one hundred years may become less of a choice for more and more people.

In 2012, the number of stepfamilies in North America (Canada and the US) exceeded the number of original families!

Stepfamilies/blended families are becoming more and more the norm. This makes it imperative for society to learn how to separate and divorce in a more child- and family-supportive way. The social, psychological and economic consequences of high-conflict separation and divorce is so damaging for children and families that society can no longer afford it or tolerate it. Major social changes have taken place in Ireland, particularly in the last thirty years. Already the changes taking place in our children's lives are breathtaking for us as parents. We all know that denying or ignoring these changes does not make them go away.

Ireland is a very small country and we all know some member of some family who has suffered separation and divorce. Divorce is here to stay and as a society we need to find a way to manage the process of separation and divorce in a more family-focused and supportive manner. We cannot continue to hurt ourselves and our children in high-conflict divorces. It is important to remember that research has shown that it is the conflict associated with the divorce that is damaging to the children, not necessarily the divorce itself. Our ability as parents to manage our divorce well is vital to our children; our ability to engage in our own healing during and after divorce, our ability to move forwards in an effective co-parenting relationship and (if desired) to enter into a new relationship are of crucial importance to our children.

The mental, physical and psychological health of our children depends on the loving nature of the family in which they are raised and, consequently, the welfare of our society depends on the mental, physical and psychological well-being of its citizens. It is vital for us as members of society and for the various organs of society when faced with the reality of a family in crisis to, first and foremost, ensure that all the appropriate support systems are made available to that family in an effort to resolve the crisis within the original family structure. If the original family cannot be saved, then it is vital to provide the resources necessary to assist that family to experience a well-managed separation/divorce, healthy ongoing co-parenting relationships and ultimately (if chosen) a loving and successful stepfamily. Society's investment in supporting the family in this way is a vital investment in the health of the nation.

As a society we are skilled in understanding the effects of death and we have traditionally recognised the benefits of the extended family and 'the village' in raising a child. Applying these skills to separation and divorce would make an immediate difference. We need to take the concepts of judgement and failure out of relationship breakdown and prioritise the concepts of love and support. In Ireland we are new to blended/stepfamilies and we need to develop a loving environment for our evolving family structures.

It is important to give children lots of time and space to develop new relationships in a stepfamily/blended family. Establishing relationships does not happen overnight. Children need plenty of reassurance and support, and a safe environment to openly voice their feelings without fear of judgement or upset. They also need to be reassured that they will have lots of access and visiting time with their other parent.

A few practical steps to help ease a child into the new relationship might include the following:

• The stepparent might start off more as a friend than a disciplinarian.
• The biological parent might remain largely responsible for control and discipline until such time as the stepparent has developed a more stable relationship with the child/children.
• The adults need to support one another. They could make a list of family rules and the stepparent can then support

these rules without being the direct disciplinarian.

The adults need to be open and clear as to their new roles. They need to resolve their feelings and concerns about any previous marriage so that old baggage, expectations or disappointments will not be brought to the new relationship. The couple need to do the work necessary to make a new, fresh and healthy start.

Try to do the following:
• Reassure the children that the divorce was not their fault. Invite the children to speak openly about any questions or concerns they may have.
• Discuss the possibility of a new family with your child long before your remarriage.
• Assure your child that he/she will continue to have an ongoing relationship with their other parent.
• Make time to talk together and listen to all the child's anxieties and worries.
• Have a unified parenting approach that is applied equally to everybody in the family.
• Make sure that you spend time alone with each of your children and stepchildren.
• Give time to your new spouse. It is important not to neglect your marriage.
• Do get help. Blending two families can be very challenging.

Try not to do the following:
• Push your children into being happy and creating relationships. Allow time and space for this to develop.
• Expect your stepchildren to call you Mammy and Daddy. Either let them decide what to call you, or decide together.

- Don't fight in front of the children.
- Do not engage with your child from a position of guilt. Be aware that if you do, you are easily manipulated by that child.

(Dr Susan Gamache's learned paper 'Introducing a New Metaphor for Separation, Divorce and Remarriage' was of great help to me in compiling this chapter.)

Top Ten Tips to Hang on the Fridge

1. Try to keep well and healthy – take exercise.

2. Take care of your children – stick to established routines.

3. Respect and support your children's need to love and have access to both their parents – support generous access.

4. Respect and support your children's need for hands-on physical, psychological, emotional and financial support and security – willingly engage with your children and willingly provide financial support.

5. Work hard at establishing a respectful ongoing co-parenting relationship with your ex-partner – it really is worth the effort and your children deserve it. Remember that you each chose the other to be the parent of your children.

6. Do not involve your children in your disputes.

7. Do not bad-mouth your ex-partner to your children (openly or subtly) and do not let anybody else do so. Ask your family and friends to constructively support you in reassuring your children of the love of both parents and in developing a healthy ongoing co-parenting relationship.

8. Get good professional help for yourself.

9. Get good professional help for your children.

10. Do not despair – you will get through this.

(Note: These ten tips are given on the assumption that you and/or your children are not in danger. If in danger, take immediate steps to get professional help.)

Appendix A

Support Organisations and Registered Bodies

ADVISORY BODIES AND RESOLUTION CENTRES

The Association of Collaborative Practitioners (www.acp.ie). See Appendix C for a full list of collaboratively trained lawyers.

Cork Resolution Centre, Cork City (www.corkresolutioncentre.ie).

Dublin Resolution Centre, Dublin (www.dublinresolutioncentre.ie).

Garda Office for Children and Youth Affairs (email youthdivision@garda.ie; tel. 01 6663812/33/33/66).

HSE general information (tel. 1850 241850).

International Association of Collaborative Practitioners (www.collaborativepractice.com).

Irish Mediators Institute (www.themii.ie).

Law Society of Ireland (www.lawsociety.ie).

Legal Aid Board (www.legalaidboard.ie).

Save Ireland (www.saveireland.ie) – creating safety for women and children.

West Cork Resolution Centre, Skibbereen (www.westcorkresolutioncentre.com).

West Cork Women Against Violence (www.westcorkwomensproject.ie; helpline 1800 203136).

Women's Aid (www.womensaid.ie; tel. 1800 341900).

COUNSELLING AND THERAPY

Accord (www.accord.ie; email info@accord.ie; tel. 01 5033112).

Association for Psychoanalysis and Psychotherapy in Ireland (APPI)

(www.appi.ie; email adminatappi@gmail.com; tel. 086 7849145).
Family Therapy Association of Ireland (FTAI) (www.familythera-pyireland.com; email amdps@indigo.ie; tel. 01 2722105).
Institute of Clinical Hypnotherapy and Psychotherapy (ICHP) (www.hypnosiseire.com; email ichphq@gmail.com; tel. 021 4273575).
Irish Analytical Psychology Association (IAPA) (www.jungireland.com; email jungireland@gmail.com; tel. 086 3557862).
Irish Association of Alcohol and Addiction Counsellors (IAAAC) (www.iaaac.org; email info@iaaac.org; tel. 01 7979187).
Irish Association for Counselling and Psychotherapy (IACP) (www.iacp.ie; email iacp@iacp.ie; tel. 01 2869933).
Irish Association of Creative Arts Therapists (www.iacat.ie; tel. 087 9921746).
Irish Association of Humanistic and Integrative Psychotherapy (email info@iahip.org; tel. 01 2841665).
Irish Association for Play Therapy (IAPTP) (www.iaptp.net; email iaptpinfo@gmail.com; tel. 0807 2210211).
Irish Association for Psychotherapy in Primary Care (www.iappcare.com; email info@iappcare.com; tel 091 565814).
Irish Council for Psychotherapy (ICOP) (www.psychotherapy-ireland.com; tel. 01 9023819).
Irish Forum for Child and Adolescent Psychotherapy (IFCAPP) (tel. 01 2722105).
Irish Institute of Cognitive and Humanistic Psychotherapy (IICHP) (www.iichp.ie; email info@chp.ie; tel. 01 2600115).
Play Therapy Ireland (PTIRL) (www.playtherapy.ie; email ptiorg@aol.com).
Psychological Society of Ireland (PSI) (www.psihq.ie; email info@psihq.ie; tel. 01 4720105).
See also www.CounsellingDirectory.ie, which will give lots of information

for registered practitioners in your area.

PARENTING INFORMATION COURSES
Barnardos National Office
Christchurch Square
Dublin 8
Tel 01 4530355; callsave 1850 222300
Email info@barnardos.ie

Community and Family Training Agency
Tel 01 8832134
Website www.cafta.ie; email: infor@cafta.ie

Cork Counselling
The Hazelton Clinic Ardfallen Medical Centre
Douglas Road
Cork
Tel 021 493 6006
Email info@corkcounselling.ie
Website www.corkcounselling.ie

Family Resource Centres and the HSE offer regular Parenting Skills
classes, Parents Plus courses and Parenting When Separated courses.
These courses are run in different areas throughout the country.
Tel 086 172 1902
Email admin@parentsplus.ie
Website www.parentsplus.ie

Help Me to Parent
10 The Lawns
Temple Manor
Celbridge

Co. Kildare
Tel 087 6890582
Email info@helpme2parent.ie
Website www.helpme2parent.ie

One Family
2 Lower Pembroke Street
Dublin 2
Tel 01 6629212
Helpline Lo-call 1890 662212
Email info@onefamily.ie
Website www.onefamily.ie

Parenting Skills Online
Website www.parentingskillsonline.com

Parenting Support (for courses in County Kildare and west Wicklow)
Website www.parentingsupport.ie

Practical Parenting
Ramleh
89 Adelaide Road
Glenageary
Co. Dublin
Tel 086 8759086
Email info@practicalparenting.ie
Website www.practicalparenting.ie

Schooldays.ie
Website www.schooldays.ie

Triple P – Positive Parenting Programme
Website www.triplep.net

Appendix B

Costs Package for Collaborative Practice

As an example, this is the package prepared by the Association of Collaborative Practitioners in Cork, the Cork Resolution Centre and the West Cork Resolution Centre for a Collaborative Divorce/Separation. These costs are valid for 2013/4.

Two-Coach Model

1. *Lawyers*

Preparation meetings – two 1-hour meetings
Collaborative meetings – five 1½-hour meetings
Pre-meeting planning sessions – five half-hour meetings
Draft documentation and prepare for court – 3½ hours

Subtotal	€3,500.00
VAT @ 23%	€805.00
Total	€4,305.00

2. *Coaches*

Client screening and preparation for process – two 1½-hour meetings each
Planning session and collaborative meetings – three meetings of 2 hours each
Support meetings – five meetings of 2 hours each

Subtotal	€1,900.00
VAT	Nil_____
Total per client	€1,900.00

Total cost per client, including 1 and 2 above   €6,205.00

If Financial Neutral or Child Specialist is required, estimated additional cost:

Child Specialist – four meetings of 1 hour each   €600.00
Financial Neutral – three meetings of 1½ hours each   €900.00
VAT @ 23% (Financial Neutral)   €207.00

Sub-total   €1,707.00
(Note: VAT was applied only to the Financial Neutral in this example.)

ONE-COACH MODEL

3. *Lawyers*
Preparatory meetings – two meetings of 2 hours each
Preparation for collaborative meeting – five meetings of ½ hour each
Collaborative meetings – five meetings of 1½ hours each
Drafting and ruling – 3½ hours

Sub-total   €3,500.00
VAT @ 23%   € 805.00
Total   €4,305.00

4. *Coach*
Screening – four meetings of 1½ hours each
Preparation and coaching meetings – six meetings of 2 hours each
Preparation for collaborative meetings – five meetings of ½ hour each
Collaborative meetings – five meetings of 1½ hours each

Total   €4,200.00

Cost per individual client –   €2,100.00
Total cost per client, including 3½ of 4 –   €6,405.00
If Financial Neutral or Child Specialist is required, the estimate is as above.

COURT PRICES

It is very difficult to endeavour to put a price on separation/divorce court proceedings as the costs depend on the level of conflict and the number of court appearances necessary. It is difficult for any solicitor, in total good faith, to tell you how much your separation/divorce will cost in court. One possible way to give a price structure is to set out a package which includes certain specified services which can be obtained at a defined price. Additional services, if required, can be priced individually or in an additional package and added to the first price as necessary. In my own practice I have endeavoured to set out some clear pricing structures for the assistance of my clients.

Appendix C

Collaboratively Trained Lawyers
(as per ACP website November 2013)

CARLOW
Kate Craig; Athy Road; Carlow; 059 9140888; admin@pjbsolrs.com

CORK
Macaire Adams; 42 South Main Street, Bandon, Co. Cork; 023 8841322; madams@pjodriscoll.com

Celine Barrett; 66A South Main Street, Bandon, Co. Cork; 023 8844211; cbarrett@bandonsolicitors.com

Eamonn Carroll; 54 North Main Street, Cork; 021 42705181 /0872353760; ecarroll@nlcc.ie

Helen Collins; Market Street, Skibbereen, Co. Cork; 028 21177; helen.collins@wolfe.ie

Noel Doherty; 6 Lapps Quay, Cork; 021 4279800; noeldoherty@fltzol.com

Mary Dorgan; 96 South Mall, Co. Cork; 021 4276556; marydorgan@securemail.ie

Peter Groarke; 12 South Mall, Cork; 021 4802700; peter.groarke@rdj.ie

Ken Heffernan; City Gate, 2nd Floor, Building 1000, Mahon, Cork; 021 24090251/087 9963334; ken@kenheffernan.ie

Kieran McCarthy; 11/12 Washington Street, Cork; 021 4275220; kmccarthy@kmccarthysolicitors.ie

Kieran O'Callaghan; 21 South Mall, Co. Cork; 0214271004; koclaw21@eircom.net

Liam O'Donovan; Upper Bridge Street, Skibbereen, Co. Cork; 028 40865;

lodsols@eircom.net

Maria O'Donovan; Market Street, Skibbereen, Co. Cork; 028 21177; maria.odonovan@wolfe.ie

Maeve O'Driscoll; 41 South Main Street, Bandon, Co. Cork; 023 8841322; modriscoll@pjodriscoll.com

Aileen O'Leary; Exchange House, Main St, Ballincollig, Co. Cork; 021 4214639; aileen@kgs.ie

Helen O'Reilly; Legal Aid Board, 5th Floor, Irish Life Building, 1A South Mall, Cork; 021 4275998; corksouth@legalaidboard.ie

Lillian O'Sullivan; 48 Maylor Street, Cork; 021 4274711; lillianosullivan@gmail.com

Teresa O'Sullivan; 6 Lapps Quay, Cork; 021 4275220; tosullivan@kmccarthysolicitors.ie

Anne Marie Sheridan; The Mall, Riverside Way, Midleton, Co. Cork; 021 4632429; info@jamesasheridan.ie

Catrina Solan; 58 South Mall, Cork; 021 4277788; cso@ofx.ie

Albert Wolfe; Main Street, Innishannon, Co. Cork; 021 4810027/086 0667875; albertwolfeandco@gmail.com

Co. Donegal

Máirín McCartney; New Row, Donegal town, Donegal, DX 74002; 074 9721753; mmccartney@gmcclaw.ie

Co. Dublin

Mary Bergin; 57 Parnell Square West, Dublin 1; 01 8727655; mbergin@faganlaw.com

Ann-Marie Blaney; Units 6-8 Blanchardstown Business Centre, Clonsilla Road, Dublin 15 – DX 99007; 01 8200455; axblaney@legalaidboard.ie

Audrey Byrne; 2 Harbourmaster Place, IFSC, Dublin 1; 01 8290000; audrey.byrne@mccannfiIzgerald.ie

Gavan Carty; 47/48 Parnell Square, Dublin 1 01   8658800;   info@kentcarty.com

Gearoidín Charlton; The Wave Building, Bulloch Harbour, Dalkey, Co.

Dublin; 01 2302157; info@charltons.ie

Kerry Clear; 42 St Stephen's Green, Dublin 2; 01 6445777; info@clearsolic-itors.ie

Hélène Coffey; 223 The Capel Building, Mary's Abbey, Dublin 7 – DX 200223; 01 8726946; hcoffey@coffeyassoc.ie

Sean Cregan; 9 Lower Ormond Quay, Dublin; 01 8724133; spcregan@legalaidboard.ie

Dillon Brendan; Unit A1 Nutgrove Office Park, Rathfarnham, Dublin 14; 01 2960666 086 2648280; brendandillon@dillon.ie

Claire Doherty; 20 On Hatch, Hatch St Lower, Dublin 2; 01 6445800; cdo-herty@IavellecoIeman.ie

Paula Duffy; Dublin; 01 4784070/01 4784895; pd@pauladuffy.com

Ray Gilmore; 22 Bridge Street, Ringsend, Dublin 4; 01 6677170; info@gilmoresolicitors.ie

Mary Griffin; 24 Ely Place, Dublin 2; 01 6766211; mary.griffin@johncwalsh.ie

Emma Heron; Riverside Two, Sir John Rogerson's Quay, Dublin 2; 01 4180600; e.heron@beauchamps.ie

Katherine Irwin; 42 Castle Street, Dalkey, Co. Dublin; 01 2849034; kather-ine@irwinsolicitors.ie

Fiona Kelly; 69 Church Street, Skerries, Co. Dublin; 01 8105799; info@fmkellyandcompany.com

Pauline Kennedy; 3 Drummartin Road, Goatstown, Dublin 14; 01 2993100; pauline@paulinekennedysolicitorcom

John Landy; 4 Talbot St, Dublin 1; 01 8746077/01 8746398/087 2517752; jkl©canninglandy.ie

Richard Lee; 5F Nutgrove Office Park, Rathfarnham, Dublin 14; 01 2960931; richard@leeandsherlock.ie

Ailbhe Levingstone; Suites 234–236, The Capel Building, Mary's Abbey, Dublin 7; 01 8732411; alibhelevingstone@oconnorbergin.ie

Josepha Madigan; 167 Lower Kimmage Road, Dublin 6W; 01 4921111/086 8164900; josepha@madigans.ie

Sharon McElligott; 69 Patrick St, Dún Laoghaire, Co. Dublin; 01 2303266; smce@mmce.ie

Jason A. McGoey; 67 Beechwood Avenue Upper, Ranelagh, Dublin 6; 01 4979864; info@jamcgoey.ie

Elizabeth McGuinness; The Gables, Skerries Road, Rush, Co. Dublin; 01 8430082; info@emcguinnesssolrs.ie

Colm Murphy; Unit 13A Main Street, Ongar Village, Dublin 15; 01 6402714/087 6791534; colm.murphy@ongarsolicitors.com

Rachel Murphy; 39/40 Upper Mount Street, Dublin 2; 01 6610866; rmurphy@lkshields.ie

Jennifer O'Brien; South Bank House, Barrow Street, Dublin; 01 6145000 /086 823898; jobrien@mhc.ie

Shauna O'Gorman; 12A Foxrock Manor, Foxrock, Dublin 18; 01 2542915; shauna@shaunamvogorman.com

Joan O'Mahony; 6 Clonkeen Road, Deansgrange, Co. Dublin; 01 2892487; info@mahonysolicitors.com

Mary O'Neill; 12 Carysfort Avenue, Blackrock; 01 2882100; info@onregan.ie

Gayle Patton; Unit 32c Rosemount Business Park, Blanchardstown, Dublin 11; 01 8293939; info@gdpatton.com

Aidan Reynolds; 4 Upper Ely Place, Dublin 2; 01 6610317; ar@gallaghershatter.ie

Tom Rowley; Main Street, Rathfarnham, Dublin 14; 01 4906577; Tom.rowley@doyleassoc.net

Eimear Sampson; 51/52 Fitzwilliam Square, Dublin 2; 01 6445800; eimearsampson@gmail.com

Christina Sauer-Dechant; Sunlight Chambers, 21 Parliament Street, Dublin 2; 01 6772353; csd@hanahoe.ie

Geraldine Shanley; 50 Fitzwilliam Square, Dublin 2; 01 6449900; gshanley@danielspring.ie

Michael Sheil; Dublin; 01 2881150; michaelsheil@eircom.net

Ken Smyth; 1–3 Fitzwilliam Street Lower, Dublin 2; 01 6425670/086 2583945; kensmyth@kensmythandco.ie

Grahame Twoomey; 2 Harbourmaster Place, IFSC, Dublin 1; 01 8290000; postmaster@mccannfitgerald.ie

Muriel Walls; Riverside One, Sir John Rogerson's Quay, Dublin 2; 01

6071217; 086 2306253; muriel.walls@mccannfigerald.ie

CO. GALWAY

Deirdre M. Brophy; The Square, Gort, Co. Galway; 091 631022; dbrophy@larkinsolicitors.com

Connie Healy; Salthill, Galway; 087 2570944; conniehealy@eircom.net

Sheenagh McCarthy; Loughrea, Co. Galway; 091 841529; law@fgmaccarthy.com

Aine Feeney McTigue; 1st Floor, Lismoyle House, Merchants Road, Galway; 091 534200; aine@feeneysolicitors.com

Brid Manifold; 9 Francis Street, Galway; 091 562480; bxmanifold@legalaidboard.ie

Pauline O'Reilly; 7 St Francis Street, Galway; 091 568129; manager@poreillysolrs.ie

CO. KILDARE

Geraldine Carthy; Market Square, Kilcullen, Co. Kildare; 045 432188; gcarthy@reidystafford.com

Helen Coughlan; Charlotte Street, Newbridge, Co. Kildare; 045 431542; helen.coughlan@pjf.ie

Lorna Duffy; Town Centre House, Naas, Co. Kildare; 045 899458; lduffy@wao.ie

Ann Nowlan; 31 Main Street, Newbridge, Co. Kildare; 045 432382; anowlan@burnsnowlan.ie

Eoin O'Connor; 16 Main Street, Naas, Co. Kildare; 045 875333; eoin@eoconnorsolicitors.ie

Susan Webster; Suva House, Main Street, Maynooth, Co. Kildare; 01 6292200; info@susanwebsterandco.ie

CO. KILKENNY

Mary Tobin; Marsh's Street, Thomastown, Co. Kilkenny; 056 7793840; mary@tobinsolicitors.ie

CO. LOUTH
Padraig Duffy; 49 Laurence Street, Drogheda, Co. Louth; 041 9839411
pwduffy@eircom.net
Paddy Goodwin; 21 Laurence Street, Drogheda, Co. Louth; 041 9837477;
paddygoodwin@eircom.net
Catherine MacGinley; Ivy House, Roden Place, Dundalk, Co. Louth; 042
9332238/087 9049111; info@mgq.ie

CO. MEATH
Annie Walsh; High Street, Trim, Co. Meath; 046 9431202; awalsh@reganm-
centee.ie

CO. SLIGO
Claire Gilligan; Teeling Street, Sligo; 071 9162855; claire@kellyryansligo.com
Keenan Johnson; Teeling Street, Ballymote, Co. Sligo; 071 9183304; john-
son.johnson@securemail.ie

CO. TIPPERARY
Ronan Kennedy; St Michael Street, Tipperary town; 062 51184; ro-
nankennedy@kfos.ie
Susan Mullins; St Michael's, Waterford Road, Carrick-on-Suir, Co. Tipperary; 051 640352; smullins@treacymullins.ie
Catherine Ryan; Friars Court, Abbey Street, Nenagh, Co. Tipperary; 067
34181; cmryan@legalaidboard.ie
Oliver Ryan; 3B Anglesea Street, Clonmel, Co. Tipperary; 052 70557; hes-
linryan@eircom.net

CO. WATERFORD
Fiona Gillen; Parade House, South Parade, Waterford; 05 874352;
info@nqg.ie

CO. WESTMEATH
Yvonne Hennessy; 14 St Loman's Terrace, Mullingar, Co. Westmeath; 044

9344854 yvonne.hennessy@hennessyandco.ie

Veronica Ann Kelly; 1 Chapterhouse, Friars Mill Road, Mullingar, Co. West-meath; 044 934841; rhona.kelly@kcs.ie

CO. WEXFORD

Annette McCarthy; Slaney Place, Enniscorthy, Co. Wexford; 053 9233547; amccarthy@folco.ie

CO. WICKLOW

Deirdre Burke; Proby House, St Mary's Road, Arklow, Co. Wicklow; 0402 24370; info@dmburke.ie

Patricia Carroll; 9 Delgany Park, Delgany, Co. Wicklow; 01 2873162; triciacarroll@imagine.ie

Peter Doyle; The Farm House, Blessington, Co. Wicklow; 045 851980; peter@collaborativesolicitors.ie

Bernadette Goff; 11 Eglington Road, Bray, Co. Wicklow; 01 27650081/086 3893333; bernie@bernadettegoff.com

Edmund Louth; Ferrybank, Arklow, Co. Wicklow; 0402 32809; edmund@cjlouthandson.ie

Paul McKnight; Church Road, Greystones, Co. Wicklow; 01 2874341/086 8344235; paul@feltonmcknight.ie

Conor Maguire; Blacklion House, Greystones, Co. Wicklow; 01 2016380; conor.maguire@conormaguire.ie

Joseph Maguire; 2 Main Street, Putland Road, Bray, Co. Wicklow; 01 2862399; info@maguiremcneice.com

Doirin Mulligan; 5 Carlton Terrace, Bray, Co. Wicklow; 01 2761707; info@rosemarygantly.ie

Catriona Murray; 1st and 2nd Floor, 95 Main Street, Bray, Co. Wicklow; 01 2868211; catriona@davidobriensolicitors.ie

Liam O'Brien; 21 Quinsboro Road, Bray, Co. Wicklow; 01 2866024; info@lobsolr.ie

Stefan O'Connor; 3 Prince of Wales Terrace, Bray, Co. Wicklow; 01 2746700; stefan@cullentyrrell.ie

Fiona Roche; 34 Vevay Road, Bray, Co. Wicklow; 01 2862150; froche@ireland.com

Maeve Roche; The Bridge, Enniskerry, Co. Wicklow; 01 2868044; mrochesolc@eircom.net

Margaret M. Roche; The Bridge, Enniskerry, Co. Wicklow; 01 2864044; mrochesolc@eircom.net

Barbara Smyth; Wicklow Law Centre, Bridge Street, Co. Wicklow; 0404 66166; basmyth@legalaidboard.ie

Glossary

Affidavit of means – A document setting out everything you own, including any houses/farms, stock, savings, your monthly income, insurance policies, stocks and bonds, investments, car, pension, etc., and also setting out everything you owe, including mortgages, bank loans and all your monthly bills. It is important that you include everything. It is a sworn document, which means when you sign it you are swearing that the contents are true and include everything you own.

Affidavit of welfare – A document which sets out all the information about your children, including their names, ages, class in school, health, ability, needs and special needs, your parenting arrangements and the housing you provide.

Barring order – An order preventing one partner from entering the family home (even if he/she is the owner) or from using or threatening to use violence or putting the other partner and/or children in fear.

Bereavement curve – Dr Elizabeth Kübler-Ross pioneered methods in the support and counselling of personal trauma, grief and grieving, associated with death and dying. Her findings, notably the 'Five Stages of Grief' model (denial, anger, bargaining, depression and acceptance), are also transferable to personal change and emotional upset resulting from factors other than death and dying, particularly in separation and divorce.

Capital Acquisitions Tax (CAT) – This is a tax on gifts given during the donor's lifetime and on inheritance following the disponer's death. There are tax-free threshold amounts which vary depending on the relationship between the person making the gift (in life or in death) and the person receiving the gift or inheritance. Spouses enjoy the highest tax-free thresholds. Since the introduction

of the Civil Partnership and Certain Rights and Obligations of Cohabitants Act 2010, civil partners now enjoy the same high thresholds as spouses.

Civil partnership – Two persons of the same sex may register their partnership under the law as set out in the Civil Partnership and Certain Rights and Obligations of Cohabitants Act 2010. The registration of their partnership affords them the protection of a significant number of rights set out in the 2010 Act.

Cohabitation – This means living together. Certain limited rights have been given to cohabitees in the Civil Partnership and Certain Rights and Obligations of Cohabitants Act 2010, provided the cohabitants qualify under the Act.

Collaborative practitioner – A solicitor or barrister who has completed training in Collaborative Family Law Practice. This also includes coaches, child specialists, accountants and financial advisers who have completed collaborative training.

Deed of transfer – A document which transfers property from one person to another.

Deed of waiver – A document where one person renounces any rights which he/she might have in a certain property.

Financial compensation order – An order of the court requiring one spouse to provide insurance cover and benefits for the other spouse.

Injunctions – An order of the court directing a person to do or to refrain from doing a particular thing.

Judicial separation – A decree/order granted by a court which relieves the spouses of a marriage of the obligation to cohabit. Each party may live as a single person but the marriage is not dissolved and they do not have the right to remarry.

Juvenile liaison scheme – An alternative to prosecution for young offenders. A juvenile who is admitted to the programme may be given an informal or a

formal caution by the Garda Juvenile Liaison Officer, usually in the presence of the juvenile's parents/guardians. The aim of the programme is to prevent young offenders from entering into the full criminal justice system by offering them a second chance.

Legal aid, Civil (includes Family Law) – Legal Aid and legal advice is provided to persons who satisfy the financial eligibility requirements and who pay a contribution to the Legal Aid Board towards the costs.

Legal aid, Criminal –The assistance of a qualified lawyer, which a person accused of a serious charge is entitled to, in the conduct of his/her defence, the cost of which is paid by the state from public funds.

Legal Aid certificate – On assessment of a person's eligibility, the Legal Aid Board will issue that person with a Legal Aid Certificate confirming that they qualify for legal aid.

Lis pendens – A registration of an action/claim against a landowner; a notice of the claim is registered in the Property Registration Authority.

Maintenance order – An order of the court which provides for the payment of weekly/monthly sums of money by one spouse to another. It may also provide for the payment of weekly/monthly sums of money for the support of the children, whether the parents are married or not.

Mediation – A voluntary process of dispute resolution in which a qualified independent third party assists the parties to the dispute to reach a settlement.

Pension adjustment order – A court order earmarking and designating a portion of a retirement benefit of a spouse (who is a member of a pension scheme) for payment to a dependent spouse and children.

Property adjustment order – An order which the court may make in respect of

property, in judicial separation or divorce proceedings; e.g. transferring property from one spouse to another or to a child.

Protection order – When a person makes an application for a barring order or a safety order, the court will make an order directing the other responding party not to interfere, harm or put in fear the applicant. It is a criminal offence to contravene this order.

Restorative justice – Restorative justice is a way of dealing with victims and offenders by focusing on the harm arising from the crime and resolving the underlying problems which caused it. It also focuses on finding ways that offenders can make things right for victims and others affected by the crime. It involves communities and victims directly and it explores ways in which the offender can be held accountable, take responsibility for their behaviour and, where possible, put things right.

Safety order – An order directing the responding partner not to use or threaten to use violence or put in fear the applicant partner and/or the dependent children or not to watch or interfere with them. It does not bar the responding party from the family home.

Service of documents – This is the formal delivery of documents to the party on the other side of the action/claim. It is usually done by registered post (to provide a provable record) and sometimes must be done personally by a person acting as a summons server.

Substituted service – If a party refuses or fails to accept delivery of documents by registered post, an application can be made to the court for permission to send the documents by ordinary post.

Succession rights – The Succession Act 1965 gives particular succession rights to a surviving spouse. Attention must be given to these rights in any separation/divorce proceedings.

References and Works Cited

1. Many papers and workshops, particularly the 'Train the Trainers' study course and back-up material, which is prepared and provided by the many wonderful teachers in the International Academy of Collaborative Professionals based in Phoenix, Arizona, USA.

2. Dr Susan Gamache, 'Introducing a New Metaphor for Separation, Divorce and Remarriage'.

3. Jennifer Tull, 'One Lawyer's Theory about Understanding Human Motivation to Increase Negotiation Effectiveness', in *Collaborative Review* 2008.

4. Henry Murdoch, *Murdoch's Dictionary of Irish Law*, Tottel Publishing 2000.

5. Dr Elizabeth Kübler-Ross, *On Death and Dying*, Routledge 1969.

6. Bernard Gaulier, Judith Margerum, Jerome A. Price and James Windell, *Defusing the High Conflict Divorce: A Treatment Guide for Working with Angry Couples*, Impact 2007.

7. Diana Mercer and Katie Jane Wennechuk, *Making Divorce Work: Eight Essential Keys to Resolving Conflict and Rebuilding Your Life*, Penguin 2010.

8. Forrest S. Mosten, *Collaborative Divorce Handbook: Helping Families Without Going to Court*, Jossey Bass 2009.

9. Pauline H. Tesler and Peggy Thompson, *Collaborative Divorce: The Revolutionary New Way to Restructure Your Family, Resolve Legal Issues and Move on*

with Your Life, Harper Collins 2006.

10. Stuart G. Webb and Ronald D. Ousky, *The Collaborative Way to Divorce: The Revolutionary Method that Results in Less Stress, Lower Costs and Happier Kids – Without Going to Court*, Plume Books 2006.

11. Nancy J. Cameron, *Collaborative Practice: Deepening the Dialogue*, Continuing Legal Education 2004.

12. Sharon Ellison, *Taking the War out of Our Words: The Art of Powerful Non-Defensive Communication*, Bay Tree Publishing 2002.

13. Marianne Williamson, *A Return to Love: Reflections on the Principles of a Course in Miracles*, Harper Collins 1992.

Index

acceptance 3

access 5, 17, 36, 37

accountants 28, 50, 56, 57

affairs 3–4

affidavits of means 35, 49, 50, 53, 56

affidavits of welfare 49, 50

aggression 14

alcohol 6, 44, 46

anger 2, 4, 8, 43

appearances 49–50

art therapy 45–6

Association of Collaborative Practitioners 21, 53

auctioneers 28, 50

bargaining 2

barring orders 32

barristers see lawyers

bereavement process 1–6

blended families 62–6

brainstorming 9–11

capital acquisitions tax 12

case progression examinations 50

child abuse 29

child specialists 26

children

    access to 5, 17, 36, 37

    co-parenting 4, 5, 16, 17, 18, 37, 44, 47, 63, 67

    custody of 37

    difficulties experienced by 43–7

    financial support for 35–6

    legal guardianship of 33, 36

    need for relationship with both parents 4, 5, 16, 17, 18, 37, 67

    and new partners 40, 41, 42, 64–6

    not criticising partner to 6, 15, 16, 17, 18, 47, 67

    professional help for 45–6, 47, 67

    removal from Ireland 32, 33

    safety of 31, 32, 37

    and stepfamilies 64–6

    supporting 2, 6, 15–18, 43–7, 67

    telling them about separation 15–18

    well-being primary consideration of court 29, 37

Children and Family Relationship Bill 36

Children's Referendum 36

Circuit Court 28, 29, 56

Civil Partnership and Certain Rights and Obligations of Cohabitants Act 12–13

civil partnerships 12

coaches 9, 25–6, 53, 56

cognitive behavioural therapy (CBT) 60–61

cohabiting 12–13, 33, 36
collaborative lawyers 25–6, 53–4, 56
collaborative practice 21, 22, 24–6, 53–4,
        56–7
communication difficulties 8, 13, 20
constructive desertion 11
control 10
co-parenting 4, 5, 16, 17, 18, 37, 44, 47,
        63, 67
Cork Mediation Service 27–8
Cork Resolution Centre 27
costs
        collaborative practice 25, 26,
        53–4
        court proceedings 29
        and legal aid 30
        mediation 28
counselling 4–5, 8, 45, 60–61
court applications 31–4, 35–8
court proceedings 19–21, 23–4, 26, 28–
        30, 48–53, 56
custody 37

decision-making 2, 8–11, 14, 24, 29
deeds of transfer 55
deeds of waiver 55
defences 49–50
denial 2
Department of Justice 33
depression 3
discovery applications 50
District Court 32, 35, 36, 37
Divorce Civil Bills 49, 52–3
Divorce Orders 52–3, 54, 55, 56, 57
Divorce Referendum 52
domestic violence 31, 32
Domestic Violence Act 32
drinking 6, 44, 46

drug abuse 44, 46
Dublin Resolution Centre 27

exercise 6, 67
extended family 41

family
        blended 62–6
        extended 41
        support from 4–5
family home
        attempts to sell or raise loans
        on 32, 33
        law relating to 7–14
        judgements registered
        against 32, 33–4
        as part of settlement 30
        valuations 28, 50
Family Law Act 48
Family Law (Divorce) Act 48
Family Resource Centres 47
family systems therapy 61
fear 2, 8, 10, 13–14, 20, 24
financial compensation orders 12
financial dependence 13
financial specialists 9, 26, 53, 56
flooding 8
friends, support from 4–5

Gardaí 32, 33, 46
general practitioners (GPs) 45
grief 3
Guardianship of Infants Act 37
guilt 2–3, 4, 66

Hague Convention 33
healing 59–60
health 5, 6, 46, 61, 63, 67

Health Service Executive (HSE) 45, 46–7
High Court 28
Home Assistance Officers 36

infidelity 3–4
inheritances 52
injunctions 33
interests 10–11, 14, 20
Irish Association of Creative Arts
    Therapies 46
Irish Association for Play Therapy and
    Psychotherapy 46
Irish Association for Psychotherapy in
    Primary Care 46
Irish Mediators Institute 21

joint custody 37
joint guardianship 33, 36
joint parenting see co-parenting
Judicial Separation and Family Law
    Reform Act 48–9
Judicial Separation Civic Bill 48–9
Judicial Separation Orders 52, 54, 55, 56,
    57
Juvenile Liaison Officers (JLOs) 46

Land Registry protections 33, 34
Law of Equity 12
Law Society of Ireland 21
lawyer-assisted mediation 27–8, 55–6
lawyers
    choosing 19–22
    collaborative 25–6, 53–4, 56
    and court applications 31–4,
    35–7
    and court proceedings 26, 28–
    9
    and legal aid 29–30, 32

and mediation 27–8, 55–6, 57
legal advice 5, 14, 25, 31–4, 54–5, 57
legal aid 29–30, 32
Legal Aid Board 22, 29–30, 32
Legal Aid Certificates 32
legal costs see costs
legal guardianship 33, 36
listening 13, 14, 18, 44

maintenance 35–6
maintenance orders 12, 13
mediation 9, 20–21, 22, 27–8, 54–6, 57
Mediation Bill 20–21
mental health 5, 6, 61, 63
moving forward 59–61

new partners 39–42, 59–60, 62–6
'no fault' separations 48–9

parenting support courses 46–7
pension adjustment orders 12, 13, 55
pension rights 12
personal development 60
physical health 5, 6, 46, 63, 67
play therapy 45–6
positions 10–11, 14, 20
power 10
probation officers 46
proper provision 20, 51–2
property see family home
property adjustment orders 11, 12, 13
protection orders 32
psychotherapy 45, 46, 60–61
PT Ireland 46

qualified cohabitants 13
reacting 8, 14
revenge, desire for 4

safety orders 32
Separation Orders see Judicial Separation Orders
Social Welfare Office 3
solicitors see lawyers
stepfamilies 62–6
succession rights 12
suicidal thoughts 3
Supreme Court 48–9, 52

tax 12

ultimatums 14

valuations 28, 50
violence 31, 32, 37

West Cork Resolution Centre 27

yardstick of equality 51, 52